the great
cultures of
Mesoamerica

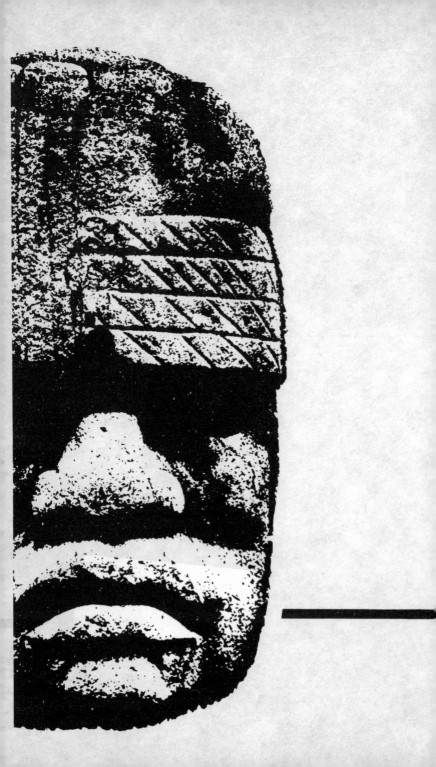

the great cultures of Meso-américa

from man's arrival on the
American Continent to the last
of the Prehistoric Cultures

Demetrio Sodi M.

PANORAMA EDITORIAL

THE GREAT CULTURES OF MESOAMERICA

Cover:
Drawing: Heraclio Ramírez

Photographs:
Irmgard Groth
I.N.A.H.

Drawings
José Narro

Translated by:
David Castledine

First edition in english: 1991
First reprint: 1993
© Panorama Editorial, S.A.
   Leibnitz 31, Col. Anzures
   11590 México, D.F.

Printed in Mexico
Impreso en México
ISBN 968-38-0280-X

index

INTRODUCTION

The great historical systems, products of the thinking of two notable historians — Oswald Spengler in "The Decline of the West" and Arnold J. Toynbee in "A Study of History" — are well-known. Since they were published, both have provided models for many historians to follow. Spengler's work appeared in 1918 (vol. I) and 1922 (vol. II), and it is interesting to recall that the author's prologue to the first (German) edition, written in Munich in 1917, closes by saying: "All that remains is to express the hope that this book is not completely unworthy of the military efforts of Germany". However, it must be pointed out that Ortega y Gasset in the first Spanish edition (Chile, 1935) speaks eloquently of the author and compares him to Eintein and Uxkül in the sense that all three share the feature of having absolute autonomy within their disciplines. He comments how Spengler compares cultures — the nine cultures referred to in his book — to plants in having a determined life-cycle: they pass through the stages of youth and maturity to fall inevitably into decrepitude.

Toynbee for his part makes an analysis of civilizations in his monumental six-volume work of which the first three appeared in 1933 and the remaining three in 1939. His well-known system states that civilizations begin to develop in response to the challenge of nature and almost always end in self-destruction.

All this is not useless erudition. Although in the case of the first author Mexican archeology had hardly begun, it had already achieved spectacular results: there was the badly excavated but imposing Pyramid of the Sun at Teotihuacan; Manuel Gamio was applying stratigraphic techniques in Azcapotzalco and excavating the Citadel (Ciudadela) at Teotihuacan in a highly scientific manner; in addition there was an enormous body of both indigenous and European information, Post-Conquest but referring to Pre-Columbian cultures, and Prescott had already published his "History of the Conquest of Mexico". Despite this, Spengler hardly mentions the Aztecs and Mayas at all.

Toynbee, who in the years he was engaged in his work must have become acquainted with the by then impressive discoveries relating to Mesoamerica, among them the deciphering of the Maya Calender, one of the most spectacular achievements of the human intellect, considers the Andean, Maya and Aztec cultures as hardly on the threshold of civilization and as not having had enough time to destroy themselves.

But the truth is that although almost completely unknown, full of mysteries but about to open itself to the Universe, extraordinarily rich in human interest, there stood pre-Hispanic Mesoamerica.

In time ethnocentric views like those of Spengler and Toynbee have been continually improved on. Without a doubt, anthropology has made a great contribution to cultural history in two main aspects by showing that:

1) Every culture is no more than the result of a composite development that derives mainly from the elements composing its own past or from those it has borrowed from other cultures.

2) Every culture tends to develop a distinctive, coherent and self-aware organization that has a propensity to absorb new elements, whether foreign or indigenous, and modify them according to its own pattern.

Within this framework of theory, how different the past appears to us. There is however yet another way to approach the history of the Continent of America, suggested by the man considered to be the father of American historiography (not of history, but of the *philosophy* of history), Edmundo O'Gorman in his book "La Invención de America" (The Invention of America).

The book takes a well-known event as its point of departure; Columbus, in the last decade of the XVth Century encountered (not discovered) islands and terra firma to the west of Europe. This event, and others that followed are the facts to which most historians limit themselves. Not so O'Gorman, who delves into the world of ideas, the ideas that give meaning to facts.

Thus, the writer unfolds a historical drama of thought. He shows the development of the background, beginnings and alternative ideas concerning this fact (the new lands being discovered) and that they were created by those who acted: Columbus, Vespucci, primarily sailors and cartographers.

But neither of them *discovered* the being or historical reality of these new lands.

Columbus said: "This is Asia, the source of Paradise". Vespucci on the other hand created another type of image with which he invented *his* reality of these lands.

The greatest obstacle of all that the so-called discovery faced was the thought that predominated in the West of those times. It was extremely difficult to accept the existence of another continent, a new one that broke the reflection of the Holy Trinity embodied in the three known ones. So extraordinary was the change in the order of ideas then prevailing that (once again) there was no alternative but to *invent* a new, wider and more liberal image of the Cosmos.

In his work Gamio demonstrates the ontological process "that gives the fact of the new lands to the west of Europe its own historical being". This historical being, smashing the old categories of western thinking is precisely the invention of America.

Embryonic America in its dual dimension of space and time had to be presented in two great sections or parts. On the one hand, the geographical invention, culminating in the publication of *"Cosmographiae Introductio"* (1507) in which the land of Américo (America) is conceived and presented as a new entity: the fourth *continuum,* the Fourth Continent.

On the other hand there is the historical invention, the determination to give a meaning and a historical destiny to this meaningless continent. For the European, America, being the new world, was potentially an old world, a field where the cultural achievement of old Europe could be surpassed.

America, then, was to be made into another Europe and so the indigenous cultures were left aside. But paradoxically, if America were to realize its historical being completely as a new Europe, at that moment its peculiar American quality would disappear.

This is the core of the ontological process that led to the invention, not the discovery, of America.

So, both the *modus generandi* and the *modus vivendi* of history must be examined, which supposes an original and deep philosophical consideration of history with universal range.

An outline of the core of this philosophical concept would be the following.

In the world of culture there are no "formed existences" that preexist concretely in themselves dispensing with all knowledge or action on the part of man. Thus it is impossible to acquire a knowledge or "discovery" of the essence or reality of such existences through simple external and factual contact.

This even happens in the physical sphere, but is more evident in that of culture, where man organizes and gives meaning to facts that are not in themselves defined.

When hitherto unknown facts intrude upon or come into contact with a human being (or a people) he initiates an ontological process with the express purpose of making these facts understandable for him. This he does by giving them a determined meaning and historical being.

He begins this process with ideas and categories that he already possessed in his intellectual equipment. Sometimes reality, acting as spontaneous dialectic, simply rejects them and renders them inoperative. In this case the process then takes on a new course, and by trial and error, he invents a new idea capable of giving sense to the facts in question. This happened in the case of America.

There is no other way but to try a new ontological process to discover America's real being, not the one that has been invented for it. A good starting point is to try to get to know as well as possible, the Mesoamerican cultures that existed, among others, on what Columbus was later to call the American Continent. This is what we hope to do in this small book, that of course is not for specialists, but a brief (and for this reason), necessarily incomplete introduction to the *Mesoamerican world*.

Though there are numerous original passages by the author, and he is entirely responsible for the arrangement and order given to the material he has used, the book is a result of compilation from bibliographical sources—but, we do believe, of the most notable specialists in the study of America. We have tried to include all of them in the bibliography but if unfortunately one has escaped notice, it was never the author's intention to use his works without due credit being given.

We also wish to make clear something that is not usual in writings on these subjects. We have always tried to combine information provided by pure archeology with that given by history, both indigenous and European, so that it will not simply be taxonomic or descriptive, as so often is the case.

We hope that it will be enriched by the thoughts and views of the creators, or their heirs with their own view of history; or perhaps, although it may sound contradictory, with their own particular "invention".

The First Steps

According to the dates most generally accepted nowadays, man began to enter the American Continent in 40,000 B.C. Originating in South Central Russia, and not in Siberia as was previously believed, he reached the ice-covered regions of the Kamchatka peninsula, the Bering Sea and crossing the Aleutian Islands, set foot on the Continent.

There has been much speculation about the reason man of those distant latitudes had for undertaking this vast program of migration. Whatever they were, the fact is that he arrived in the future America where he had to find a different response to nature's challenge. He had to create new cultures, different from the ones that developed in Europe; cultures of no less value, simply different but with flashes of genius and exceptional intellectual attainments that were equaled in Europe much later or never.

Making use of the polar ice-cap that in this geological era, the Pleistocene, stretched as far south as Wisconsin, U.S.A. (and for this reason the era is also known as the Fourth or Wisconsin Glacial Stage), man established various migration routes that remained more or less the same until much later.

The two best-known routes seem to have re-united at their extreme southern limits. One runs down the Pacific Coast and the other strikes into the interior as far as the Great Lakes.

For a time the first route came to an end in the southwest of the United States, and the second in the east. After absorbing numerous influences that gradually arrived with new settlers, the two routes run south where a fusion of ethnic groups, languages, cultural traditions, including of course technical knowledge and skills, gave rise to the beginning of the cultural development that was to create Mesoamerica.

This may be an oversimplified explanation of what happened in those far-off times. However, it is enough for what is to be studied later and helps to give a background, that if very simplified, is nonetheless generally accepted by authorities. But before we can talk about Mesoamerica, there is more to say about this prehistoric man.

One, perhaps obvious, point to be made is that man was arriving on the Continent in various and more or less continuous waves from 40,000 B.C. onward, and not of course in one single migration. There is at present data indicating that small groups of individuals were still entering the Continent as late as the XIIth century A.D., just before the Conquest, in fact.

Another point worth underlining is that these small groups, arriving late and almost certainly by chance, produced no effect on the indigenous development of the American cultures.

In spite of the assertions of the diffusionist theory or of the most recent and absurd one of extraterrestrial beings, we believe that the American cultures evolved by themselves and are completely indigenous.

However, it must not be supposed that man entered the continent only via the Bering Strait. There are well-founded theories about other migratory waves from areas such as Melanesia and Polynesia. At the same time, these have no paleontological support approaching that of the Bering Strait theory, and secondly refer rather to either possible influences in North America or to the settling of South America. These theories will therefore be set aside as they do not concern our subject, Mesoamerica.

The man that arrived in America was already *Homo-Sapiens*. Among the culture traits he possessed was more or less complex lithic tradition and clothing based on animal skins; he was familiar with fire, had primitive hunting weapons and equally primitive methods of fishing and food-gathering.

In fact, we still know little about such remote epochs, but we can be sure that in his migration, man was accompanied by a varied group of mammals of the Pleistocene, a fauna that included among others great numbers of animals such as the mastodon, the mammoth, the horse, the giant sloth, the wolf, the cave bear, the bison, etc., many of which have since become extinct.

By reason of these culture traits authorities speak of groups of primitive food-gatherers, nomadic hunters or food-gathering hunters. As was mentioned before, their cultural traditions included of course technology and it is on the basis of lithic industries or complexes that the experts classify these peoples.

Discoveries such as those at Lewisville, Texas; Santa Rosa Island, California; Texas Street, California; Trile Springs, Nevada; La Jolla, California, and other sites, yield Carbon 14 dating of between 38,000 and 17,000

ARRIVAL OF THE FIRST SETTLERS ON THE AMERICAN CONTINENT VIA THE BERING STRAIT

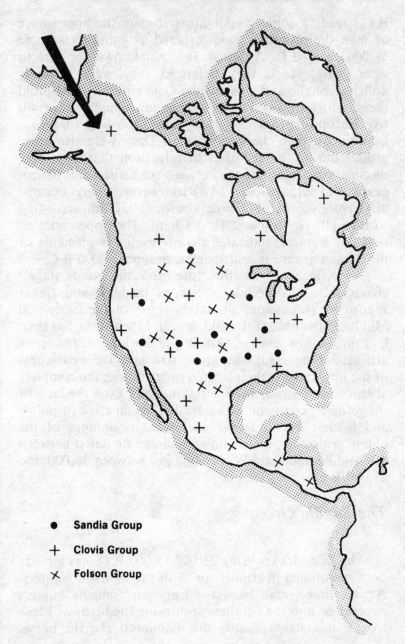

- ● **Sandia Group**
- + **Clovis Group**
- × **Folson Group**

B.C., leading some investigators to date the appearance of man the primitive food-gathered as going back some 38,000 years B.C. Although it is not known for sure to what racial stock they belonged they were certainly dolichocephalic and close to the Caucasoid or Australoid races, which means that they were quite similar to primitive Europeans (massive brow ridge, receding forehead, broad nose, high cheekbones, etc.) There were also other groups during the centuries of migration that were of a physical type intermediate between the Caucasoids (European) and Mongoloids (Asiatics) before these became differentiated to the degree known today (all according to Birdsell, Hooton and Piña Chán). The appearance of nomadic hunters, indicated mainly by the implements of the Sandía group, is a little later, around 25,000 B.C.

For Krieger, this is the "pre-projectile points stage" characterized by nodules, rounded pebbles, and flakes shaped by percussion, similar to those of the Early and Middle Paleolithic of the Old World. Much stress has been laid on the low level of skill in the working of the stone artifacts discovered; the great size and the coarseness of the implements; their limited range of use; the complete absence of finish or precise flaking, and even the lack of the refined percussion necessary for the tapering of points and blades. This stage antedates the beginnings of the oldest projectile points known and can be dated between the Middle and Late Wisconsin, i.e. between 38,000 and 23,000 B.C.

The Sandía Group

This complex covering 25,000-15,000 B.C. has already been mentioned in connection with the nomadic hunters. At this time, small bands of Eurasian nomadic hunters penetrated into the continent following the herds of Pleistocene animals, especially the mammoth and the horse.

Later came the mastodon, the giant ground sloth and the big-horned bison.

They used long lanceolate points with a lateral tang or shoulder, called Sandía points after the site in New Mexico where they were first discovered. The lateral tang and the flaking have similarities with the Gravettian and Solutrean points of Europe and Asia. Skin scrapers have also been found, with obtuse faces and narrow necks, similar to Asian examples, as have bifacial implements and remains of mastodon, mammoth, horse, bison and camel, some of them charred.

Clovis Group

Later than Sandía, the Clovis group (15,000-9,000 B.C.) shows the steps made in the technology of prehistoric American man. At that time he depended more on the mammoth, or perhaps he specialized in hunting this animal. As he roamed the high plains of the United States, he is also known as the Plains Culture.

In this phase there are fluted proyectile points, bone implements, hammerstones, burins or gravers and flake knives, generally associated with the bones of mammoth, although on the Lehner site in Arizona, bones of tapir, horse and bison were also found.

Clovis points are characteristically lanceolate, with parallel or slightly convex sides, concave base and have grooves on one or both sides produced by the removal of several longtitudinal flakes, one channel being longer than the other.

Folsom Group

The points of the Folsom group, dating from around 9,000 to 7,000 B.C. show real technical skill in their fineness and delicate pressure flaking. They are characteristically lance-shaped with a longtitudinal groove or channel on either face running from the concave base for almost the whole length of the point. This groove was obtained by the removal of a single flake, showing a high degree of craftsmanship. These points are found in association with bones of bison, which may indicate the extinction of the mammoth or a specialized hunting economy based on bison.

There are also scrapers of various types, hammerstones, stone polishers, crushers, knives made of fine flakes, stone blades, bone awls, gravers, stone and bone beads as well as some discs with decorated borders, perhaps for use as pendants. But the most important feature of all in the period is the indisputable evidence of the first use of spear-throwers, or *atlatl* as they were called by the Nahua. This ingenious instrument, that within the historic period at times reached the status of a true work of art, is still used in some parts of the Continent.

All this took place mainly (but not exclusively) in North America. What was happening in Mesoamerica around the time when Folsom terminated? This we shall see in the following chapter, together with the history of the most important plant on the Continent: corn. We shall take up the thread of history and examine fully the evolution of a period of specifically Mesoamerican prehistory.

But firstly, the other side of the coin with respect to prehistory. Not everything in history is as arid as the description of projectile points or pottery vessels. There are also myths, the first hesitant chronicles of historians and, why not, rumour.

When the Spaniards arrived in the 16th century they began to collect various stories about the giants that had lived there previously, and simply considered these to be first inhabitants of these lands.

In fact, the *Annals of Cuautitlán,* a native document drawn up after the Conquest that tells the history of the Nahua peoples, says that giants lived in the Second Age or Sun. This second Sun refers to one of the cataclysms that, according to myth, had happened through the ages before the creation of the last or Fifth Sun in which they were living.

The *History of Tlaxcala,* another native document, says that the beings that existed when the flood occured were giants, whose bones could be found scattered in ravines.

Father Arlegui states that he saw a molar in the village of San Agustín, between Durango and San Juan del Río "that was more than a «cuarta» (i.e. 21 cm.) square". Father Tello reports that a certain Francisco Océlotl from Jalisco found thirty giants, including three women, in the Valle de Tlala, six leagues from Guadalajara.

The Conquistador and historian Bernal Díaz del Castillo tells that he saw some large bones, whose size caused him to say: "We all marveled to see such huge bones, and were convinced that there had been giants in this land".

The historic Olmecs are said to have seized the territory of Tlaxcala from giants, and the Otomí considered themselves the oldest settlers, after the giants.

These giants, called *quinametin* are described by Gregorio López, Royal Physician of New Spain and personal physician to Philip II, who was sent by the King to make investigations in New Spain. López says that they were 5 meters tall.

Father Bernardino de Sahagún writes that they built the pyramids of Teotihuacan, and Father Juan de Torquemada speaks of one called *Xelhua* who built the pyramid of Cholula.

What all these observers saw or referred to were no other but the bones of the great animals of the Pleistocene, later indentified by paleontology and archeological investigations.

Only one man with an extraordinary vision of history, came anywhere near the truth: Father José de Acosta, who between 1540 and 1600 was already of the opinion that America had been originally settled by peoples from elsewhere, and wrote: "that the Indians arrived to people that country by land rather than by sea" and added that "the first to enter these lands were more wild men and hunters than civilized and refined nations".

Corn and the Tehuacan caves

Around 1945 the origin of corn was still extremely obscure. Archeology had shown that an early but not primitive form of corn existed in the Virú Valley, Peru; in the Valley of Mexico, both dating around 1,000 B.C. and in the Southeast U.S.A. dating around 500 B.C. This showed in a very general and inconclusive way that corn seemed to have been domesticated somewhere in the vast area stretching from Arizona to Peru. There was also the theory that corn had its origin in southeast Asia.

However, in 1948 and 1950 Herbert Dick discovered prehistoric vegetable material in the Bat Cave, New Mexico, that included beards and other parts of corn, lying at different levels that showed a process of evolution. The oldest samples were dated by radio-carbon analysis to around 3,600 B.C. The corn was of the "palomero" (without husk type and another with husk)[1]

In 1949 Richard MacNeish obtained samples of prehistoric corn in the Cueva de la Perra, Tamaulipas, in northeast Mexico. Here too the samples obtained from the highest to the lowest layers of cave deposit cover an evolutive series. The oldest samples were dated by radiocarbon to 2,500 B.C., and were identified as the early form of Nal-Tel.

In 1954, MacNeish and David Kelly excavated the Romero and Valenzuela caves in the Cañon del Infiernillo. The corn discovered showed similar characteristics to that from the Bat Cave, and was dated to around 2.200 B.C. It was interesting to find in the Romero cave some specimens of teosinte, which were dated to between 1,400 and 400 B.C. Traces of the same plant, dated to between 1,800 and 1,400 B.C., also appeared in human feces.

Several other excavations also produced samples of corn until in 1954 Barghoorn and others identified pollen grains of wild corn under present day Mexico City at a depth of 70 meters, corresponding to the last interglacial period, which occurred, according to present estimates, 80,000 years ago. These fossil grains of corn

---

[1] Four strains of corn have been identified for Mexico: *Palomero Toluqueño*, with substrains *Jalisciense* and *Poblano*. Found between 2,220-2,800 meters above sea level, having short or very short ears (7-11 cms.), with 20 or more of kernels.

Arrocillo Amarillo, found between 1,600 and 2,000 meters above sea-level, with very short ears (5-7 cms.) and an average of 15.4 rows of kernels.

Chapalote, up to 1,800 meters above sea-level; short or medium ears (12-15 cms.) and an average of 12.3 rows of kernels.

Nal-Tel, originally from Guatemala but extending into Mexico. Found up to 1,800 m. above sea-level, with short ears (9-10 cms.) and an average of 11.4 rows of kernels.

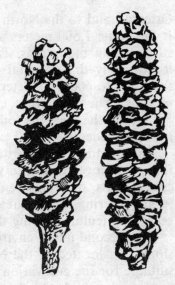

*Samples of primitive corn
found in the caves
of Tehuacán, Puebla.
The drawing of the sample
is exactly life size.*

pollen proved that the plant is American and that the ancestor of corn is maize and not one of its related species, teosinte or gama grass.

These discoveries considerably reduced the area in which the origin of corn was to be sought. At last, in 1960 MacNeish made a preliminary exploration in the Tehuacán Valley, Puebla, and discovered beards of corn that were at first thought to be wild. At last a crucial zone had been reached.

Characteristics of the Tehuacán Valley

The Tehuacán Valley is located in the South of the State of Puebla and the most northerly part of the State of Oaxaca on the Central Plateau of Mexico. MacNeish concentrated on an area 40km. by 30km. This Valley is surrounded in the South and East by the Sierra Madre

Oriental, and to the North and West by the Mixtec Knot. It lies some 1,500 meters above sea-level, and due to the surrounding mountains, is in a rainshadow that makes it extremely dry. Annual precipitation ranges from less than 500 to 600 millimeters, occuring in a period of two months. The vegetation consists mainly of xerophytes.

Within the area, the following five micro-environments have been identified:

Firstly, the "Valley with alluvial bottom", a relatively flat plain covered at intervals with mesquite, cactus and coarse grass, offering the possibility of both hunting and food gathering during the dry periods, and primitive wet season agriculture during the rains.

The second micro-environment, known as "Travertine slopes" is located in the Northwest of the Valley and is suitable for the cultivation of corn and tomatoes and for hunting deer and rabbit during the wet season.

The third is the "Thorn wood of Coxcatlán", in the East, South and Southwest of the Valley, yielding seasonal wild fruit, whitetail deer, rabbit, skunk and peccary.

The "Eroded Canyons" within the "Thorn wood of Coxcatlán" are inexploitable except by a very limited number of persons during the rainy season. Both this region and the following "El Riego", are sub-zones. "El Riego" is an area of streams to the North and West of the town of Tehuacán, with relatively abundant vegetation and numerous animals. This zone can be exploited all year round employing primitive techniques of subsistence.

In general, the Valley is capable of supporting a limited population, nomadic in conformity with the seasons, or a larger population if techniques such as agriculture, irrigation, etc., have been developed.

This area was investigated by a large group of experts. Archeological survey resulted in the discovery of 454 new sites or prehistoric dwellings ranging from small campsites to great urban ruins. Test trenches were dug on 30 of these sites, and 12 in another revealed deeply stratified remains and showed 140 sedimentary layers and occupied zones. Enough data was obtained from these to make a broad reconstruction of the ancient inhabitants' way of life and they also yielded information on their subsistence, food habits, diet, climatic changes and even evidence concerning the months of the year during which the sites were occupied. 23,600 specimens of dessicated corn were obtained, that furnished the evidence necessary to clarify the origin and evolution of the plant.

Let us now summarize the culture traits of five of the nine phases and cultural horizons that have been identified in the valley of Tehuacán.

Ajuereado Phase

Radio-carbon dating indicates that this phase seems to have terminated in 6,500 B.C., and could have begun some three or four millenia before. The population was grouped in small nomadic families, changing their camps three or four times a year following the seasons. They were food-gatherers and hunted horse and antelope, although their meat was mainly of hare, mole, rat, tortoise, birds and other small mammals.

The vegetation was probably xerophytic and the preliminary studies of pollen and animal bones indicate that the climate was somewhat colder and wetter that now.

The implements were few, and all flaked from flint: knives, leaf-shaped projectile points flaked bi-facially, scrapers, flake and bi-facial choppers, burins and prismatic blades.

In a word, as most of the remains of the animals that were trapped or hunted at this period are small, and there is no evidence of big-game, man of the Ajuereado phase must be considered as belonging to the cultural stage of plant and animal collector.

"El Riego" Phase

Radio-carbon analysis indicates that this phase developed betwen 6,500 and 4,000 B.C.. People were nomadic, but there was a population growth and they appear to have changed their settlement patterns. They subsisted mainly on the plants and animals that they collected, supplemented by products of hunting very similar to those of the Ajuereado phase, although deer was hunted instead of horse and antelope, and rabbit in place of hare. There was no fundamental change in hunting and trapping, but plant-gathering was more important than in the preceding phase.

Hence it can be inferred that in this phase the idea was conceived that by dropping a seed into the ground, a plant would result. Thus people seem to have domesticated the avocado and a variety of squash, while at the same time they gathered wild plants such as cotton, chili, amaranth and corn, which they finally domesticated.

The development of settlement and subsistence patterns almost certainly brought about changes in their social organization. They may have been patrilineal clans with some concept of territory and perhaps the shamans or sorcerers appeared later, though not as fully-fledged specialists.

The production of implements changed and increased, and projectile points appear with a narrow blade and concave base, delicately flaked and used as darts from the *atlatl* or spear thrower for hunting. The large scrapers, the blades and burins of the preceding stage persist.

The use of polished and smoothed stone begins; mortars and pestles and also querns make their appearance. These mortars may have served to modify the way food was prepared.

There are, however, two more important developments: weaving and carpentry (nets, textiles, woven baskets, pieces of spear shafts and traps) and evidence of relatively elaborate burials, indicating possible beliefs and complex ceremonies. In one of the burials discovered were the skeletons of two children. One had been ceremonially incinerated, and the head of the other had been separated and charred, the brain extracted, and then placed in a basket on the child's chest.

Another burial included an adult man, an adolescent girl and a child less than one year old. There was evidence that the man had been intentionally burnt, and the heads of both the girl and the child crushed, perhaps on purpose. In both burials, the bodies were wrapped in coarse cloth and nets, and in association with basketwork.

"Coxcatlán" Phase

This lasted from 4,900 to 3,500 B.C., and thus derives from the El Riego phase. The way of life must have been almost the same as in the El Riego phase. Small nomadic groups in the dry season, and large ones in the wet season. The latter groups seem to have been larger than in the preceding phase and stayed on the same site for longer periods.

The folk of Coxcatlán continued to be basically food-gatherers and hunters, but acquired more domesticated plants such as corn, chili, avocado and gourd, followed later by amaranth, common bean, squash, the black and the white zapote (zapodilla). These plants formed approximately 10% of the diet.

The small groups or microgroups perhaps sowed some domesticated plants in spring, and as the number of these grew, man could live in macrobands for longer periods. When his agricultural reserves ran out he returned to nomadic microgroups.

There were changes in the patterns of settlement and subsistence and consequently in social organization. The groups probably remained patrilineal, but "rights of property" must have been more clearly defined, and the shaman became more powerful as he attended to rites connected with agriculture.

Different types of projectile points with flanges make their appearance; blade knives are made with more care, new types of cutters and scrapers appear, real querns with handstones replace mortars and pestles, and progress was made in the manufacture of nets, spirally woven bags and textiles.

The most characteristic feature of this phase is the incipient agriculture.

"Abejas" Phase

This phase is calculated to have lasted from 3,500 to 2,300 B.C. The main changes that took place are related to settlement patterns, shown by the discovery of ten hunting camps occupied by macrogroups during the dry season, while another eight settlements of macrogroups seem to have been used for a longer period. There are also some which must have been occupied all year round, which was made possible by the improvement of agricultural techniques and the greater efficacy of food production. To the plants already known were added domesticated canavalia, another type of squash, tepary bean and some varieties of hybrid corn with introgression of teosinte, although more than 70% of the diet still consisted of wild plants and animals.

The same artifacts continued to be used, although some types are a little different and new ones were created that carried over into the following periods.

The new artifacts were open-wave basketwork, stone bowls and globular jars, saddle querns, obsidian blades fashioned from long cylindrical cores, and other objets.

The most important feature of this phase is the early domestication of wild corn, and the cultivated corn found belonging to this period has been called "early trip-

sacoid", a term describing any combination of characteristics that could have been introduced into corn by hybrid-
ization with its near relatives, teosinte and gama grass.

As neither teosinte nor gama grass are known nowadays in the Valley of Tehuacán and are not represented
in archeological remains, it seems that tripsacoid corn
was introduced from some other region, possibly the basin
of the Río Balsas in the neighboring State of Guerrero,
where both teosinte and gama grass are common.

"Purrón" Phase

Dating between 2,300 and 1,500 B.C. this is the least
clear phase as only two living areas are known. In general
the materials are the same as in the preceding phase, but
an extremely important step forward is made: pottery
appears, that is the oldest yet found in Mesoamerica. The
forms follow those of the stone bowls and globular jars
(ollas) of the earlier period, although both this pottery
and the stone recipients at Tehuacán cannot be the first to
be made in Mesoamerica, but are probably imitations of
an older type of pottery as yet undiscovered, of some other
area.

This is a point at which to stop because the Purrón
phase falls clearly in the Preclassic period, which must be
analysed apart, together with the Olmecs. But first, we
now have a basis on which to understand what Mesoamerica is.

Mesoamerica

We now have sufficient data to try to define what Mesoamerica is. As we have seen, man ceased to hesitate and doubt before nature's challenge. Gradually he has laid down the foundations of his cultures that in the future he would carry forward into classic civilization and a period within written history. But these two periods, on much superior levels, evolved in only two of the great areas of America: Mesoamerica and the Andean Zone.

The other great superareas, that never reached the same degree of development are those of primitive and advanced agriculturists, the hunters of the East and West U.S.A., the advanced agriculturists of the Chibcha region in the South of Mesoamerica, and lastly in the Amazon. Let us examine this more closely.

Mesoamerica is our subject. What does this concept mean, what does it represent for us, and from what point of view? In actual fact, Mesoamerica is both a geographical and a cultural concept, but to arrive at this concept a long period of speculations, hard thinking and attempts at conceptualization that were never really adequate, was necessary.

Most Americanists simply divide the continent in the easiest way into North and South. Some insert another section between the two: Mexico and Central America, the so-called Middle America. And yet this is not exactly the same thing as Mesoamerica. If the continent is divided into north and south, the commonly accepted bio-geographical line of division is formed by the San Juan river, between Nicaragua and Costa Rica. If Mexico and Central America are considered, this includes the territory lying between the northern border of Mexico and the eastern border of Panama. Middle America is more or less the same, but sometimes excludes northern Mexico, and at others includes the Caribbean. Incidentally, the term Middle America, as used by American antropologists is not original. In the last century the term "Mittel Amerika" was used by the German anthropologist Eduard Seler with the same meaning.

But obviously, these divisions are of no or very little use for the anthropologist who wishes to characterize culture areas or establish zones of mutual influence. For example, according to the first division, cultures such as *Sumo, Misquito, Paya,* and *Jicaque* fall within North America, when in fact they are as "Southamerican" as the *Chibcha* and the cultures of Central America. In the south there is no homogeneity, since there are such different cultures as the *Caribs, Fuegians* and *Incas.*

Moreover, discounting the north of Mexico, the cultures that developed in the southern part of the country and in Central America have nothing "Northamerican" about them, but have traits that place them nearer to South America, although they are quite distinct.

There is another division or geographical classification. Some anthropologists, taking cultural levels as a base, divide the indigenous cultures of America into the five following groups:

1) Food-gatherers, hunters and fishers of North America.
2) Primitive farmers of North America.
3) Advanced farmers ("higher cultures")
4) Primitive farmers of South America.
5) Gatherers and hunters of South America.

This division is much more useful, but it must be remembered that within the vast areas occupied by the groups belonging to these five cultural levels, there are also subareas of lower cultural levels that are surrounded by and live alongside the predominant culture. These are kinds of "subareas" within "superareas". Thus, for example among the primitive farmers of North America, the "southeast" and "southwest" would be superareas, within the zone of advanced farmers we can define a vast superarea which since 1943, thanks to Paul Kirchhoff, the theorist of the area, has been called Mesoamerica. Since that time we have had, finally, a term or concept, or more correctly, a superarea whose geographical confines, ethnic composition and cultural characteristics allow us to delineate and therefore study more deeply a region that stands out against the other cultures of the Continent and which deserves to be investigated apart.

Before going on however, one thing must be made clear. Kirchhoff's Mesoamerica is that of the 16th century. It is easy to see why he confined himself to this epoch. We have abundant written information for the 16th century and from this we can extract data with which to define the geographical, the ethnic and the cultural aspects. In addition, we have much more data from the many archeological excavations that have been made in the superarea.

It must remain clear that we here refer to Mesoamerica as defined by Kirchhoff in 1943. Later, with the progress made in excavations (that have had a spectacular boom) some investigators have proposed modifications, mainly in respect to the northern frontier, although they almost always reffered to pre-16th century frontier. It also must be said that if we wish to delimit. Mesoamerica before the 16th century it will be increasingly difficult because as we go back in time, scientific evidence becomes scarcer and scarcer, and the problem more and more complex.

Ethnic composition of Mesoamerica

According to Kirchhoff, the human groups existing in Mesoamerica in the 16th century can be grouped into the following five categories

1)   Tribes speaking languages as yet unclassified such as *Tarascan, Cuitlatec, Lenca* and others.

2)   All the tribes of the *Maya, Zoque* and *Totonac* linguistic families. According to some investigators the languages of these three families, to which *Huave* should probably be added, form a group which can be called *Zoque-Maya* or *Macro-Mayance*.

3)   All the tribes, except two, of the *Otomí, Chocho-Popoloca* and *Mixtec* families that with the *Chorotegamangue* family, seem to form a group called *Otomanguean;* and all the tribes of the *Trique, Zapotec* and *Chinantec* family, considered by others to be related to the former group, comprising a large group called *Macro-Otomanguean.*

4)   All the tribes of the *Nahua* family and a series of other tribes of *Yuto-Aztec* affiliation, in-

cluding the *Coras* and *Huicholes,* whose grouping into families is still not definitive.

5)   All the tribes of the *Tlapaneca-Subtiaba* and *Tequistlatec* that belong to Sapir's *Hokano* group.

So, according to Kirchhoff, analysis of the ethnic composition of 16th-century Mesoamerica based on the above demonstrates the following:

a)   Only one of the linguistic families forming Mesoamerica, *Otomí,* has some members (the *Pame* and the *Jonaz,* which may in fact be two subdivisions of the same tribe), which do not belong to this cultural group.

b)   Two linguistic groups formed by some of the families mentioned, the *Zoque-Maya* and the *Macro-Otomanguean,* should their existence be proved, would be contained wholly in Mesoamerica.

c)   Tribes of these two groups, and also of the *Nahua* family reach, probably as a result of migrations, the ultimate geographical limits of Mesoamerica, both in the north (the *Huastecs* of the *Zoque-Maya* group; the *Otomí* of the *Macro-Otomanguean;* and the *Cazcán* and *Mexicanos* (= Aztecs) of the *Nahua* group) and the south (the *Chol-Chortí* of the *Zoque-Maya* group; the *Chorotega* of the *Macro-Otomanguean;* and the *Nicarao* of the *Nahua* family).

As has been pointed out, we are referring to what Kirchhoff said in 1943, and restated in 1960. At present however, various experts do not completely agree with these analyses, but this is a problem which we cannot examine in detail here.

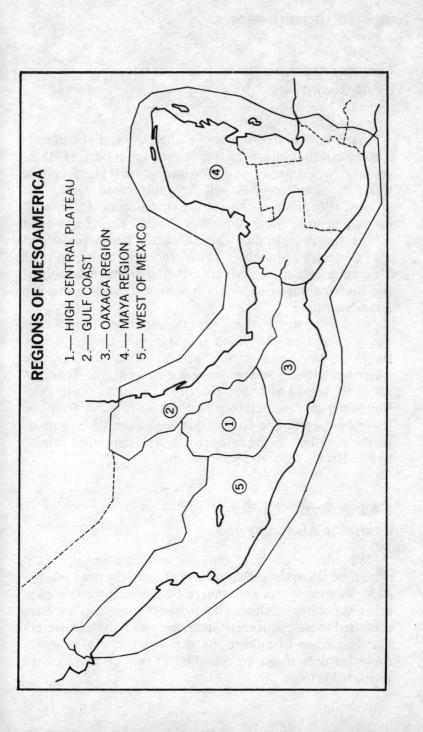

REGIONS OF MESOAMERICA

1.— HIGH CENTRAL PLATEAU
2.— GULF COAST
3.— OAXACA REGION
4.— MAYA REGION
5.— WEST OF MEXICO

Geographical Limits
of Mesoamerica

With the help of the above analyses and the indent-ification of the culture traits proper to the superarea, 16th-century Mesoamerica could be delineated. These culture traits or characteristics will be enumerated later. The groups of Mesoamerican culture that occupied the south in that century were the *Chol-Chortí,* the *Lenca* (and maybe the *Matagalpa),* the *Subtiaba,* the *Nicarao* and the *Chorotega-Mangue.* Thus, the southern limit of Mesoamerica can be fixed as running from the north of the River Motagua to the Gulf of Nicoya, passing through Lake Nicaragua.

As for the north, there were the *Huastecs,* the *Mexica-nos of Meztitlan,* the *Otomí* and *Mazahua,* the *Tarascans,* the *Coca,* the *Tecuexe,* the *Cazcan,* part of the *Zacateca* (there were food-gatherer-hunters *Zacateca),* the *Tepehua-nos,* the *Acaxee* and the *Moacrito.* The northern limit of Mesoamerica can therefore be fixed as running from the River Pánuco on the Gulf of Mexico to the River Sinaloa on the Pacific, passing through a central depresion formed by the Rivers Tula and Moctezuma.

Characteristic Culture
Traits of Mesoamerica

We shall enumerate only the principal ones, but it should be understood that several of them are not exclusive to Mesoamerica but were shared by other ethnic groups in other superareas. Although Kirchhoff does not, we have classified these cultural elements according to the different manifestations of culture, its use, context, etc. Some of these features could be classified in two or more of the proposed groups.

Religion and ritual

Cosmogony and Cosmic vision: Several creations and destructions of the world; 13 or 19 cycles, the earth and 9 underworlds:

A complex pantheon of deities presided over by a dual god or pair of divinities associated with the creation of the world.

Fixed and movable religious feasts.

The use of two calendars: one solar of 365 days and another ritual of 260, with combinations of the two to form a cycle of 52 years.

Wooden drum with two tongues.

Ritual Cannibalism.

Confession of moral transgressions.

Use of paper and rubber.

Flying-pole game.

Steam bath.

Human Sacrifice.

Burning people alive and extraction of the heart.

Flaying alive.

Sprinkling sanctuaries with the blood of sacrificial victims.

Autosacrifice.

Blood letting from the tongue, ears, legs and sexual organs.

Dancing dressed in the skin of a sacrificially flayed victim.

Quail sacrifices.

13, 4 and 9 used as ritual numbers.

Writing

Hieroglyphic writing.

Use of numerals with a relative value according to position.

Folded books (codices).
Historical Annals and maps.

Socio-political organization

Patrilineal clans of the *Calpulli* type.
Military Orders (eagles and tigers).
Merchants acting simultaneously as spies and ambassadors.
Organization into social classes—Nobility, priests and macehuales (coomon people).
Specialized markets or markets subdivided according to specialties.

Technology

Polishing of obsidian.
Copper tubes to drill stone.
Rafts with gourd floats.
Use of the comal (griddle) to cook tortillas.
Metallurgy.
Proyectile points of various materials; awls, scrapers, burins, spindle whorls, plumb bobs and polishers.

Architecture

Constructions in stone or clay.
Stepped pyramids.
Stuccoed floors and walls, often in polychrome or with mural paintings.
Ball courts with rings.
Paved avenues.
Hanging bridges.
Underground ovens.

Warfare

Wooden swords edged with flint or obsidian chips.
Shields with two handgrips.
Head trophies.
Lances.
Clay pellets for blowguns.
Use of bow and arrow (also for hunting).
Wars for the purpose of obtaining sacrificial victims
(Flower War).

Agriculture

Use of the *coa* or digging stick.
Chinampas, or the construction of gardens by reclaiming land from lakes.
Cultivation by hand.
Cultivation of corn, chili, bean; chía (lime-leaved sage) for use in beverages or for an oil to give luster to paints; century plant (maguey) for its juice (aguamiel), syrup, pulque, paper, and thorns for autosacrifice; cacao, sweet potato, cotton, yucca, pineapple, avocado, papaya, zapote and varieties of plum.
Grinding of corn softened with ashes or lime (nixtamal).
Irrigation.

Paraphernalia

Use of rabbit fur to decorate textiles.
Cotton corselettes.
Turbans.
Sandals with heelguards.
One-piece suits for warriors.
Lig plugs, ear plugs, necklaces, bracelets, anklets, pectorals, frequently made of precious metals.

Chronology of Mesoamerica

Thanks to Paul Kirchhoff we have been able to situate Mesoamerica geographically and characterize it culturally, at least for the 16th century. We will now try to situate it chronologically, although in very general terms; but firstly, a few comments that will give a theoretical framework.

In Mexican Archeology we use the term "Cultural Horizons". These horizons are based on the examination of two fundamental measurements: space and time. Or as Willey says, "they are horizontal crosspieces by which the vertical columns of specialized regional developments connect with each other in a time schem."

Mexican and American archeologists working in collaboration have been able to establish a (generally accepted) Chronological Table to date the various cultural horizons. This table is general however, meaning that when more exact information is obtained from archeological zones by more thorough exploration it may not coincide with the general dates that are much more "rounded off". The table is nevertheless extremely useful.

The table has been arrived at using two criteria: stratigraphical excavations in each place, and dates established by carbon 14 or Radiocarbon. Fortunately the results give by both methods have coincided, which shows the reliability of the Chronological Table of Mesoamerica.

The first cultural phase was represented, as we have seen, by the hunters of mammoth and other extinct animals. Discoveries such as those at Tepexpan, Sta. Isabel and others indicate that more than 10,000 years ago B.C. man was hunting big game around Lake Texcoco, which at that time was larger than at time of the Conquest. Industries or lithic complexes like the one at Chalco, arrowheads and other stone implements found associated with mammoth bones prove the presence of hunters. Alfonso Caso's proposal that this phase should be called the Prehistoric Horizon was accepted.

In the second phase agriculture was invented. Discoveries such as those of MacNeish in Tehuacán give us the dates discussed in the preceding chapter. It is interesting to note that corn began to be cultivated at the same time as other cereals were grown for the first time in Palestine. Caso proposed the name of "Primitive Horizon" for this phase, but at the same time notes that it could also be called the Horizon of the Beginning of Agriculture.

The following Horizon is know as the Preclassic, in which villages and later towns began to be established. Writing, numerals written in a system of dashes and dots, the calendar and a rich and complex pantheon all appear. Shook discovered a stelae in the Altos de Guatemala which could possibly be dated at 800 B.C., and Alfonso Caso found a great number at Monte Albán, with inscriptions in their indigenous languages but with Latin characters B.C.. But both Shook and Caso found a perfectly developed calendar on these stelae, with glyphs for days, the year, the months, etc., and which necessarily must have been elaborated in a previous period. We can say, very approximately, that its development began shortly before the first millenium B.C.. Thus, the Preclassic can be situated between 2,000 B.C. and approximately the beginning of the Christian Era.

The Preclassic Horizon is followed by the Classic, which began in 100 B.C. and finished in 800 or 900 A.D. This is the phase of Mesoamerican cultures: Mayas, Zapotecs, Mixtecs, and in particular the people of Teotihuacan, among others.

The last is the Historic Horizon. We have historical information about this period, passed on by the natives as oral tradition or in Codices, and transmitted to the Spaniards, or else written down by the natives themselves in their indigenous languages but with Latin characters after the Conquest. It can be fixed as a mean towards 1520.

For this period Alfonso Caso was able to interpret the chronicles written in Codices or native documents in hieroglyphics in the Mixtec Codices, and the earliest date he found in them is equivalent to 690 A.D. There has been written history in Mesoamerica since at least the 7th century A.D.

This is the chronological development of culture in a part of Mexico and the northern section of Central America, which we call Mesoamerica. Such a simple outline is of great help in discussing the subjects to be dealt with in this book.

The Preclassic

Let us take up the thread again of the history that we left in the Purrón phase in the Tehuacán Caves. This phase falls within the Preclassic, an extremely important period since it is the last step before the great Classic flowering of Mesoamerican cultures. The Preclassic period is really very similar in all parts of Mesoamerica: all the ethnic groups occupying the area at that time used more or less the same socioeconomic systems. In other words, no group had developed any form so distinct as to merit absolutely independent consideration as a fully defined culture.

However, towards the end of the period there appears on the Gulf coast the first great culture of Mesoamerica— the Olmec, which does need to be examined apart. Therefore, although within this same period it will be given a special place in our studies.

The fact that the cultures were similar during the Preclassic does not mean of course that regional styles did not exist, that often exerted influence on each other. The period is important not only because it comes immediately before the Classic but also because it was at this time that certain structures become defined, forming what might be called a cultural substratum common to all Mesoamerica. In time, particularly during the Classic period, this became differentiated according to local developments that were so distinct that at a glance we can identify and distinguish Maya and Zapotec; Teotihuacan and Totonac; Mixtec and Huastec, etc., while at the same time discovering commong traits in all of them, those characteristic features listed in the chapter on Mesoamerica.

As we have seen, the Preclassic can be situated approximately between 2,000 B.C. and the beginning of the Christian era, but specialists, to simplify their studies, divide it into Lower, Middle and Upper Preclassic, based on the classification by type of the pottery and figurines that show the same tradition technologically. Each subdivision of the period lasts approximately 600 to 700 years.

Logically, the Upper Preclassic is the most important of the three stages; firstly of course because it is the most advanced, but also because it is in this stage that the first examples of writing and the stone calendar appear, because architecture has its beginning and because it is the moment of the Olmecs' greatest glory. Also, because the end of the period shows the earliest achievements of the Classic.

In the light of what has been said, we cannot profitably describe all the Preclassic styles found in Mesoamerica. Let us limit ourselves to the description of the Preclassic as it developed on the Central Plateau of what is now Mexico, since this is the main area of study in the book.

Clay acrobat. Middle Preclassic.
Tlatilco, State of Mexico.

Lower Preclassic.
(ca. 2,000 to 1,300 B.C.)

In order to know the Lower Preclassic of the Central Plateau we have to base our examinations on three main sites which are the oldest in the Valley of Mexico and perhaps of all Central America. These are El Arbolillo, Tlatilco and Zacatenco.

None of these three had completely risen above prehistoric techniques and way of life, but they already possessed the cultural equipment that we have seen primitive Mesoamerican man slowly develop thoughout the course of millennia. To understand how the inhabitants of these three villages or settlements lived, we must recall the conditions in the Valley of Mexico at that time.

The landscape is certain to have been extraordinarily beautiful. Towards the east lay the Sierra of Ahualco, or Sierra Nevada, from which rose the two immense snowy peaks of the volcanoes Iztaccíhuatl and Popocatépetl.

To the south, the spurs of Popocatépetl came into contact with the rugged sierra of another volcano, the Ajusco, and formed the western limit of the basin by joining the Sierra de las Cruces, La Malinche and Monte Alto and Monte Bajo.

The Sierra de Guadalupe displayed its main heights: the Cerro Gordo, the Cerro del Chiquihuite and the Cerro de Cuauhtémoc dipping afterwards in the Cuesta de Barrientos and continuing under the name of the Sierra de Tepotzotlán.

In the distance could be seen the Cerro Sincoque, the Cerro de Tezontlalpan, the Cerro de Jalpan and the metal-bearing Sierra de Pachuca, and all this huge, rocky circle was closed in the north by the Telapón and the Tlaloc, heights in the Sierra Nevada, towards the Cerro de Patlachique.

In the center of this frame lay a vast lake whose waters reached as far as land 2,245 meters above sea-level, and from which rose, in the shape of small island or promontories the Cerros of La Estrella and Chimalhuacán, the Sierra de Santa Catarina, the Peñon de los Baños, del Marqués and Xico and extinct volcanoes such as La Caldera, Xatepeque and San Nicolás.

Rainfall was abundant and this, together with the humid climate favored the growth of lush pasture and hence grasslands supporting horse, mammoth and bison. There were also numerous coniferous forests, mountain valleys with fertile alluvial deposits ideal for agriculture, abundant fish and material for gathering.

For the man of the Preclassic epoch, big-game hunting was a thing of the past, but he had plenty of scope in other directions. The three settlements occupied that magnificent countryside that deservedly made the Conquistadors exclaim that it appeared to be an enchanted vision when they saw it from the Tajon del Aguila (today, Paso de Cortés), between the two volcanoes.

The earliest settlement, El Arbolillo in the present-day State of Mexico lay very near the edge of the lake, but was also hemmed in by mountainous outcrops behind, and so must have depended more on products of the lake than on hunting or agriculture.

Tlatilco on the other hand was surrounded by the alluvial plain created by the Río Hondo and its affluents (Totolica and los Cuartos), and so agriculture was the most important for the inhabitants, though they also practiced food-gathering, hunting and fishing.

Zacatenco's position was similar to that of El Arbolillo, i.e. it lay on a hillside with the lakeshore a few yards away, and so probably depended mainly on products from the lake.

The economy of the Preclassic can be reduced to the cultivation of corn, hunting, fishing and gathering, the activities being primary or secondary according to the conditions enjoyed by each group. Let us not forget however the cultural development in Tehuacán: several plants had already been domesticated that almost certainly complemented their diet. Bones of deer and birds indicate the ingestion of animal protein in these settlements.

Similarly, they had inherited a highly developed technology that in fact underwent very little change throughout this horizon. Here the materials of the Basin were used: volcanic stone, rounded pebbles, bones and antlers of deer, obsidian, clay and perhaps wood served in the manufacture of mortars, saddle querns, handstones, scrapers, projectiles, polishers, blades, hammerstones, etc. At the same time there was some extraordinary pottery, mainly for domestic purposes, and a great variety of figurines made by a combination of two techniques, modeling and appliqué ("pastillaje") which means that small rolls or balls of clays, (often incised) were used for decoration and details such as the mouth, earpieces and eyes. According to George C. Vaillant's classification, the figurines of this period were of the types C1a, C1b, C3a, C3b, C3c, C1-2, old F and others.

These figurines often denote a fertility cult, shown by exaggerated thighs, as well as more or less developed funeral rites that, we have seen in Tehuacán, have quite remote origins. So, we find figurines buried with the bodies, that were usually placed directly in graves dug in the earth, generally in a fully extended position. The scattered graves lead to the conclusion that it was usual to bury the dead near cultivated fields or under houses.

As for pottery, that for household use predominates, especially pots for carrying water, for cooking, and storing, but there are also simple and composite silhouette bowls, plates and pitchers in which cone-shapes and round bottoms predominate. All was in monochrome: blackish or bay, polished black, polished white, pale brown and pale polished red. The decoration is geometrical and incised, running all round the vessel.

The figurines give us much ethnographic information. These people do not seem to have used textiles, a fact attested by the absence of spindle-whorls, but although generally naked, they may have occasionally used breech-clouts or loincloths. They painted their bodies and faces, perforated the earlobes and septum for earpieces and noseplugs, wore bracelets, necklaces, anklets, etc.. They used sandals of leather and perhaps of maguey fiber, painted their hair which they dressed in sometimes highly complicated ways with the help of bands probably woven or made otherwise of natural fibers.

Agriculture, favored by the fertility of the basin obliged the population to become sedentary and their houses were of straw, sticks and mud, grouped together in farming hamlets near lakes and rivers, forming a local community that seems to have been the highest level reached in socio-political organization.

It is interesting to note that woman had a very important role. She took part in the production of food alongside the men, was a potter, participated in the tasks of food gathering, preparing food and caring for children. The man, on the other hand, fished, hunted, farmed and dedicated himself to other duties. There was certainly a division of labor, since the perfection of certain ceramic pieces point to professional potter-craftsmen.

This was man and life in the Lower Preclassic.

Middle Preclassic
(ca. 1,300-700 B.C.)

Two important things happened in this period. First, the hamlets began to grow and expand until they became real townlets. In addition there was a notable cultural growth because it was at this time that Olmec influence reached the Valley, of a period that we could also call

Preclassic Olmec but which was more advanced than that of the area.

The number of settlements grew, and we find among them El Arbolillo, Tlatilco and Zacatenco once again, plus Xalostoc, Copilco, Tlapacoya, Coatepec and others. In them, the cultural equipment of the *Lower Preclassic* survives in totality, but numerous features are added such as axes and adzes for work in the fields; abraders, sharpeners, perforators, knives, bone needles, chisels, the so-named "yokes" and "stirrups", scrapers, etc., and new materials were used; jade, serpentine, hematite, quartz, turquoise, kaolin and others.

The presence of serpentine axes, the *coa* or digging stick and perhaps of wooden hoes indicate that agriculture was already carried out on the system, still widely used today, of felling, burning and clearing.

The mixed economy continued, but hunting and fishing activities increase, suggested by the plentiful representation in pottery of ducks, boars, opossums, frogs, turtles, water snakes, birds, fish, rabbits, bears, and dogs. Corn, beans and squash were grown and are also represented in art.

At the same time specialized functions became defined. As in all human cultures, the principal specialist was the shaman, and it was at this period that appears a group of people carrying out ritual functions, involved in sowing, propitiating natural forces and celebrating important ceremonies. The shaman or sorcerer proper was not the only member of the group; it also included the ball-game players, dancers, musicians, acrobats and others. Piña Chan thinks that these people acted only during festivals, but we believe that there was already specialization, that in fact had developed into professions.

Religion was possibly based on magic, that is on devices invented by man to oblige nature to act in accordance with his designs. To achieve this, symbols began to appear which finally led to writing.

Clay dancer, Middle Preclassic.
Tlatilco, State of Mexico.

Social organization this period was based on magic and the fertility cult survived, but also, thanks to Olmecs, a cult of a feline deity appears. We shall understand this better later when we study the Olmecs.

This feline deity is a kind of celestial dragon, and here is something very important for the understanding of the Toltec period which will be referred to later. Everthing seems to indicate that the aquatic serpent was a sort of water spirit for this period, but it was a serpent with a kind of crest on its head, an obvious ancestor of Quetzalcóatl.

Towards the end of the period also appears the representation of a deity that could be considered the ancestor of the god of fire, or, as Piña Chan says, a pre-god of fire, that in Tlatilco is represented as a hunchback with a bowl or brazier on his head. This representation of Huehuetéotl, the Old God, fire, remains the same up to the Conquest.

As for burial customs, they became notably more complex during this period. For example, in Tlatilco the burials are highly elaborate. There are multiple burials men with women, children with women, women with women, and dismembered children, positive evidence that human sacrifice was practiced and that it was customary to bury an important person accompanied by another. The offerings are much richer than in the preceding period, perhaps with the idea that they would be useful for the dead in an afterlife. It was also usual to sacrifice a dog and deposit it alongside the body perhaps, even as early as this, with the intention that the animal should accompany the dead person during his journey to the underworld.

Pottery generally preserves the tradition of the previous epoch, but with local variations. Thus we find various color schemes: white on red, red on white, red on brown, red on pale yellow, burnished red, thin, incised black, reddish-brown or beige, etc. But, as we have remarked, the Olmec influence also arrived, distinguished by thick black pottery with scooped-out designs, black with borders or white spots, gray or grayish, deep orange-red, deep yellowish-red, and pseudo fresco.

As for the forms, there were ollas, simple and composite silhouette bowls and pitchers, all with spherical bottoms. The Olmecs contributed bowls jugs of the Chavín (Peru) type, jugs with stirrup handles, anthropomorphic and zoomorphic vessels, generally flat-bottomed.

Incised patterns running completely round the vessels predominate. The Olmecs were responsible for the use of decoration formed by rubbing or cutting away the background; a fresco painting begins, with designs being placed in areas or discontinuously. A distinctive feature of Olmec pottery is the predominance of feline motifs, i.e. the wild cat or American jaguar (tigrillo).

The figurines of this period, according to Vaillant's classification, are of types B, C5, F and K, but also, due to Olmec influence, types A, C9, D1, D2 are found and the one called babyface, which is a distinctive feature of Olmec art.

This was the cultural expression of Middle Preclassic man in Mesoamerica.

Upper Preclassic
(ca. 700 B.C. to 100 A.D.)

In this period we can already discern what will happen later in Mesoamerica. Culture in the Valley rises to new heights, and this is without a doubt due to the influence of Olmec culture. While in the preceding period the population lived grouped in hamlets or small villages and the huts were built of perishable materials, now they began to assemble in totemic clans, which led to a class of magicians or sorcerers holding supreme power.

The hamlets become real towns, and the full-time specializations, industry and commerce, the consequent diversification of labor, specialized centers for food supplies, population, religion and socio-political organization all develop and increase notably.

There are very many sites belonging to this period in the Valley of Mexico, prominent ones being Zacatenco, San Cristóbal Ecatepec, Cerro del Tepalcate, Lomas de Becerra, Cuicuilco, Ticomán, Tetelpan, Tlapacoya, Contreras, Chimalhuacán, Papalotla, Tezcoco, Azcapotzalco, Xico, El Tepalcate, Cuanalan; Tepetla and even Teotihuacan show traits characteristic of this period. Several of these sites also became real ceremonial centers as well as settlements, which accounts for the appearance at this time of civico-religious constructions. Thus began the great architecture of Mesoamerica.

Agricultural methods are improved, larger areas are cleared for cultivation, the system of terraced fields appears but the population becomes more dependent on hunting since the Valley suffered drought conditions.

Technology is the same as in the preceding period, but with the addition of chisels for cutting stone, drills and implements of volcanic stone for polishing walls and floors.

Pottery passes from the utilitarian to the commercial stage, and begins to be sent to other areas. The production of luxury objects begins on a large scale, and with farming, hunting and fishing the picture of the specialized activities is complete.

There was a great change in religious matters. Although the sorcerer did not completely disappear he was supplanted by an incipient class of priests, intermediaries between the gods and men. The cult of Huehuetéotl, the god of fire, grows remarkably, and the first representations of the water god appear, mainly in a crude form on the necks of bottle-shaped pottery.

The cult of the dead becomes more complex and the custom arose of burying important people in stone tombs constructed inside religious edifices or in the bases of temples, or else they are placed radially as in Cuicuilco.

Pottery keeps the forms and colors of the preceding epoch, but polychrome ceramics predominate in red, yellowish brown, white and cream, sometimes with incised patterns. Distinctive features are negative painting in dark tones, ornamental mammiform, bulbous or cylindrical supports, plates with raised lips or basal flanges, high annular bases, bowl supports, pouring handles without a bridge, solid lugs, etc. There is also pottery brought from other places such as found on the Cerro del Tepalcate, where there is pottery from Chupícuaro, Guanajuato. This pottery, which is almost certain to have come down the Lerma River, is bichrome and polychrome. There are also figurines type H4, which all influenced the local pottery styles giving rise to new types, made principally in Cuanalan, Azcapotzalco, Xico and other places.

As an inevitable result of religion becoming complex, or rather finally becoming organized, great architecture made its appearance. At first, as gods were considered practically the same as human beings, temples are simply a copy of ordinary huts but, based on these lay forms, stone designs gradually develop. It is therefore impressive to see the archeological zone of Cuicuilco that possesses the oldest architectonic constructions (pyramids) not only in Mesoamerica but on the whole continent.

But not all the authorities are in agreement over this. Piña Chán says that the outstanding architectural remains of this period are those of the Cerro del Tepalcate, which shows (as does Cuicuilco) various superposed edifices or occasional reconstructions of the pyramidal base. It appears that every time the pyramid was rebuilt, the temple was burnt, perhaps as a magical protection, and a propitiatory offering was made in the base construction. According to Carbon 14, the Cerro del Tepalcate can be dated at 450 B.C.

The exploration of Cuicuilco was begun in 1922 by the University of Arizona under the direction of Byron C. Cummings, who was obliged to use explosives to remove the vitrified rocks that covered it to a depth of 8 meters. These rocks were originally formed by the lava from the eruption of Xitli, one of the cones of the Ajusco volcano. As in the case of the Cerro del Tepalcate, the pyramid of Cuicuilco was repaired and reconstructed several times, and was built on a vast artificial terrace. After the excavations, the pyramid, which had been damaged by the explosives, had to be protected by a covering of stone, altering its original shape to a certain extent, although what can be seen today is, generally speaking, what was left after the invasion by lava.

The monument as it stands now is a pyramid of four superposed terraces rising to a maximum height of about 18 meters. The base is an almost perfect circle with a maximum diameter of 135 meters. The stone facing is inclined at an angle of 45°. The sloping walls (talud) to be seen now do not belong to the last stage of the pyramid, as this was destroyed by the explosions. This can be verified by looking at the walls that are 4 to 6 meters deeper than the present ground level and are therefore the best preserved.

Up the east side ran a stairway that was impossible to reconstruct because it was in such a poor state of preservation, but up the west face ran a ramp coinciding with the axis of the stairway. On the upper part evidence was found that indicated the existence of a fifth terrace, surmounted by a rectangular structure, of which traces remain. The pyramid consists of a central nucleus round which building was carried out at various times in concentric circles, by which it is possible to identify the various periods. An interesting feature is a sort of altar that was discovered at the foot of the western ramp. It is made of superposed stone slabs that seem to form a vault and are painted with red lines, perhaps symbolizing serpents. This is not the only altar however; several others have been discovered around the pyramid.

From this important site, together with the archeological zone of Ticomán originated a cultural tradition known as Ticomán-Cuicuilco that, we shall see in the next chapter, is particularly important in the formation of the Teotihuacan culture.

This approximately was the culture and life of Mesoamerican man in the Upper Preclassic.

The Olmecs

We shall devote a long section to the Olmecs, not only because of their importance, but because a study of them in many ways synthesizes all the history of Mesoamerica.

As Wigberto Jiménez Moreno says, 1941 and 1942 can be considered fundamental for Mexican archeology. In 1941 a round table of the Sociedad Mexicana de Antropología (Mexican Antropological Society) was held in Mexico City, and in 1942 another in Tuxtla Gutiérrez, capital of the State of Chiapas. In both meetings highly interesting tropics were discussed. At the first meeting the role that the cities of Teotihuacan and Tula played, in an independent but historically linked fashion, was classified, and the error that prevailed of confusing Teotihuacan and the Tula of the Toltecs was corrected. At the second meeting the meaning of what was then rather vaguely and obscurely called "Olmec culture" was clarified and defined. As was stated on this occasion:

"The term «Olmec» means «inhabitant of the rubber region» which is par excellence the south of Veracruz and the north of Tabasco, and could therefore be applied to a succession of peoples of different ethnic and linguistic affiliation who, successively or simultaneously occupied the said region".

But, according to information given by chroniclers and historians mainly in the 16th century, there appear to have been not only Olmecs of the rubber region, but also some that occupied areas like the Central Plateau of present day Mexico. Very often these cannot be identified in any way at all with the coastal Olmecs, and it is not known whether they were called Olmecs because they originally came from the coast or because they went there to live later.

At the 1942 round table the business was rather to elucidate the problems of the archeological Olmecs who, as we have seen, began to leave their mark on the cultures of Mesoamerica as far back as the Middle Preclassic, and for this reason have rightly been called a "mother culture". It is also true that the other Olmecs, since their chronology and culture traits have not been defined, created many problems of historical interpretation. All this is pointed out by Jiménez Moreno, who prepared an analysis of the various Olmecs throughout the centuries of Mesoamerican history.

Before describing briefly the culture of the archeological Olmecs, who interest us most in this chapter about their epoch, it will be profitable to examine the historical Olmecs. For this we will follow Jiménez Moreno's example by working from the most recent to the most ancient; that is, we shall begin by talking about the Olmecs at the moment of the Conquest and finish by examining the archeological Olmecs, the Olmecs "par excellence".

The latest Olmecs mentioned by the chroniclers, in this case by Fray Bernardino de Sahagún in Book X of his *"Historia de las Cosas de la Nueva España"* (History of the Things of New Spain) are Olmecs of the coast, contemporaries of what is known as the Aztec Empire.

According to Sahagún's informants, who called them *Olmeca uixtotin mixteca,* these lived on the Gulf Coast at the time of the Conquest. They were said to speak a barbarian language, meaning that they did not speak Náhuatl, the language of the informants. But it was also said that some spoke Náhuatl too, and Sahagún identifies them with Mixtecs of the coast, i.e. the Mixtequilla region. From a 16th century document we know that in fact Mixtec was spoken in this area at the time. Here was a place called *Mixtán,* from where the *Mixtec* nation most probably came, and as Mixtec pottery has been found there, the evidence is sufficient for there to be no doubt that these Mixtecs of the informants really existed. But as we have seen, alongside these Mixtecs, lived Nahuas and also people of the Mije-Popoloca groups, whose language is still spoken in this region, while Mixtec has disappeared.

To quote Jiménez Moreno:

"The last Olmecs of the coast and of places near the altiplano were, according to this, more or less "Nahuatized" Popoloca-Mixtec tribes, alongside which lived the Chinantecs and the Mije-Popolocas who appear to represent an older stratum".

According to the historian Chimalpain, before the above mentioned peoples existed the Olmecs of Chalco-Amaquemecan, contemporary with the first Chichimec monarchs in the 13th century.

Amaquemecan, today Amecameca, lies in the skirts of the volcanoes Ixtaccíhuatl and Popocatépetl, in the Mexican Sierra Nevada. The information given by Chimalpain prove that Olmecs lived there until the year 1261, when they were driven out by invaders called *Chichimecs-Totolimpanecas* and *Tlaxcaltecs.*

These Olmecs were also known as *Xochmeca* or *Xochteca* and *Quiahuizteca,* the meaning of the last name coinciding with that of *Ñusabi,* which the Mixtecs call

Jade dwarf. Olmec culture.
Cerro de las Mesas, Veracruz.

themselves. In fact, a lord of Tlaxiaco in the Mixteca attempted to recover his rights to a vast territory stretching as far as the volcanoes (i.e. Amecameca) in the time of Moctezuma II; and in Tenochtitlan, the Aztec capital, there was a colony of Mixtecs called the *tlailotlaque* or "the returned". Some Cuicatecs (related to the Mixtecs) could remember having lived at Amecameca, and there is definite connection between Mixtec pottery and that called Aztec I and Cholultec I.

Even earlier, towards the 12th century, chroniclers speak of Olmecs at Cholula and Tlaxcala, contemporary with the destruction of the Toltec Empire. The most likely dates for the fall of Tula, the Toltec capital, are believed to be either 1156 or 1168. When the nations forming the Empire — Nahuas and Otomis — broke up, the remaining members emigrated, and are known to history as *Nahuatlaca Tribes*.

One of these tribes, the *Cholultecs* remembered clearly their Toltec origins, and through sources of information they are known to have been the *Toltec-Chichimecs,* who wandered around until they settled in Cholula as slaves of the Olmecs, living there. Finally these Toltecs attacked the Olmecs, using their own weapons, and expelled them. The homeless Olmecs had to fight against related tribes such as the *Xochimilca, Ayapanca, Texaloque* and others. In this they had help from Chichimecs related to the Otomi, therefore those *Xochimilca* seen to have been of Olmec stock, and are perhaps the *Xochimeca* who lived in Chalco-Amaquemecan. But the Olmecs proper were dispersed in two directions after being driven out of Cholula: some went to the mountains of Zacatlán in the present State of Puebla (the *Olmeca-Zacateca)* and others to the south (the *Olmeca-Xicallanca).*

As can be gathered from the above, the Toltecs after the fall of Tula, the Mixtecs and the Olmecs of Cholula were all in close contact, according to historical sources that often call them all (and others, such as the *Xochimil-*

ca), Olmecs. To explain this apparently complicated confusion of different groups under the heading of Olmecs, Jiménez Moreno puts forward the following hypothesis, using the classifications of pottery provided by archeology.

1. "Since Cholultec I and Aztec I pottery seems to have originated in the *Mixteca,* it could perhaps be attributed to the most recent Olmecs who would then be identified with Nahua-Mixtec tribes (so much so that their modern decendents would be the Nahua-speaking peoples in the south of Veracruz and also in the Zacatlán sierra where this dialect was called *Olmeca-Mexicano* in the 18th century). This would explain why there is a shared base, a common denominator for both the Toltec and Mixtec cultures. The pottery of the Cerro Montoso and the Isla de Sacrificios is closely linked to the Aztec - Cholultec I pottery, and so could represent an extension of the Cholula Olmec culture towards the coast some time after the 10th century. All of this would check with sources".

2. "According to this, both the Tolteca-Chichimeca when they established themselves at Cholula and the Culhuas (of the same lineage when they founded the new Culhuacán before the ruin of the Tula Empire), came into contact with Olmec tribes — either with this name or called Xochmeca or Xochimilca — and in dominating them nevertheless adopted their pottery styles (Aztec I-Cholultec I). This explains how, although the Tolteca-Chichimeca and the Culhuas had pottery of the Mazapan-Coyotlatelco-Matlazinca II type while they lived at Tula, they abandoned it and how the culture represented by Aztec I-Cholultec I, Mixtec pottery and that of the Cerro Montoso and the Isla de Sacrificios prevailed".

Sahagún preserves a very ancient tradition according to which some tribes arrived by sea at Panuco and lived at Tamoanchan for a long time, but one day the wise men embarked again and sailed eastward, declaring that they would return when the world was about to end. It was then that some old men who stayed behind at Tamoanchan, among them two called *Oxomoco* and *Cipactónal,* corrected the calendar. They were said to go to pray at Teotihuacan when they lived at Tamoanchan, from which it can be inferred that the cities were not far from each other. Teotihuacan, as we have seen, was said like Cholula to have been built by giants. These people would be the Olmecs of Tamoanchan, both a mythical and real place that is a place of origin but also, afterwards, a place that can be localized geographically.

Sahagún, following this tradition, says:

"And all being at Tamoanchan, certain families departed to people the provinces, who are now called *Olmeca Uixtoti,* who formerly knew curses or spells, and whose leader and lord had a pact with the devil, and was called *Olmecatl Uixtotli* from whom they took the name and called themselves *Olmecas Uixtotin.*

These Olmecs are reported to have gone in pursuit of the Toltecs when they left the city of Tullan, and went east, taking with them the pictures they used for sorcery. When they reached the port they stayed there as they could not cross the sea, and from these descended the people now called Anahuaca-Mixteca; and their ancestors settled this region because their lord was the one who chose the land as being good and rich.

These same people invented the way to make the wine of the country; it was woman who began and found out how to pierce the maguey to extract the juice from which wine is made. And this juice was called *mayauel,* and he who first found the roots that are thrown into the juice was called *Patecatl.* And the authors of the art of pulque-making, as it is carried out now, called themselves *Tepuztecatl, Quatlapanqui, Tliloa, Papaztactzocaca* all of whom invented how to make pulque on the mountain called *Chichinahuia;* and because this wine makes foam, they also called the mountain *Popozonaltépetl,* which means foaming mountain; and when the wine had been made, the aforesaid invited all the important people, old men and old women, to the mountain, where they gave them all food to eat and of the wine they had made to drink; and to each one present at the banquet they gave four cups of wine, and to no one five in order that they should not become inebriated. And there was a *Cuexteco,* who was lord and master of the *Cuexteca,* who drank five cups of wine, with which he lost his mind and in this state threw off his maxtle (loincloth) exposing his private parts, upon which the said inventors of the wine, being much embarrassed and ashamed, gathered together to punish him; however, as the *Cuexteco* discovered this, he fled out of pure shame with all his vassals and the others who understood his language and they went towards *Panotlan,* whence they had come, that is now called *Pantlan* and the Spaniards call Panuco. Arriving at the port they could go no farther, and so settled the area, and are those that now call themselves *Toneyome,* wich means in Indian (in Mexican) *Touampohuan* and in Spanish, "our fellow men"; and their name, which is *Cuexteca,* was taken from their lord and master who called himself Cuextecatl".

As will be seen, this charming text refers to highly important facts, such as the *Olmecas Uixtotin* who left Tamoanchan; the origin of the *Anahuaca Mixteca,* the invention of pulque, and the reason why the *Huastecs (Cuexteca)* occupy part of the Gulf Coast.

As for the locality of historic or geographic Tamoanchan, both Jiménez Moreno and Piña Chán are inclined to believe that it was in Morelos, and had close links with the people of Chalco-Amaquemecan. The mythical Tamoanchan to which Sahagún's tradition refers, both because of what the texts relate and because it seems the term can be interpreted only in Huastec, must have perhaps been situated in an area of the northern Gulf Coast from Boca del Río to the Huasteca, if in fact it did not include part of the Olmec territory proper, i.e. southern Veracruz and northern Tabasco.

All this is extremely important in the possible geographical identification of Tamoanchan, because it would be there that the archeological Olmecs and the historical Olmecs could have met. To repeat what has already been said, the facts seem to place it in the present State of Morelos. The author of the *Histoire du Mechque* says that the first man was created in a cave called Tamoanchan, that was in the province of *Quauhnahuac* (Cuernavaca, state capital of Morelos). These is also in this state, to the northwest of *Tepoztlán,* where the gods of pulque among them *Tepuztecatl,* used to be venerated, a hill called *Chichinauhtzin,* like the *Chichinahuia* of the text but with an honorific suffix.

Many coastal features and representations of these deities appear in the ruins of Xochicalco, in the State of Morelos. There is also a cave here like the one mentioned by the author of the *Histoire* that was adapted as an astronomical observatory. The culture of Xochicalco is partly derived from the culture of the last stage of Teotihuacan. Lastly, on the facade of the main pyramid are calendar glyphs that perhaps show a correction like the one made by *Oxomoco* and *Cipactónal.* In short, many features lead to the belief that Xochicalco is the historico-geographical Tamoanchan.

There are also other historical Olmecs called Nonoalca, about which Jiménez Moreno says: "The Nonoalca seem to be identified with the Mazateco-Popolocas, partially Nahuatized, and also to have been the last representatives of the Teotihuacan IV-V phase".

We are getting nearer and nearer the archeological Olmecs, since in the Cerro de las Mesas, an eminently archeological Olmec area, has been found an upper stratum containing *Cerro Montoso* pottery, and before this another one that corresponds to Teotihuacan III-IV. This is where the point of contact can be established.

Lastly, in his studies Jiménez Moreno cites other historical Olmecs, who are definitely linked to the archeological Olmecs. These are the Totonaca-Zoqueanos, about which he says:

"The Totonacs, according to Torquemada, claimed to have built the great pyramids of Teotihuacan, and I think that this tradition should not be completely disregarded. In my lecture on *The Teotihuacan Culture and the Chichimecs* I called attention to the similarities I have noticed between what we know of the Totonacs' religion and what can be deduced about the religion of the Teotihuacan people from the fresco on the Temple of Agriculture (apparently a little later than the Pyramid of the Sun) and the contents of a 16th century "Relación de Teotihuacán". In addition, the figuries of the *El Buzón* (Veracruz) type — that are closely related to the heads of the Teotihuacan II type — suggest certain physical characteristics that correspond with what Sahagún notes about the features of the Totonacs. Therefore, I believe that the Totonacs must have been present at Teotihuacan — whether as masters or slaves — in the earliest phases of this culture, those corresponding to heads of types I, II, and III, when the pyramids were built and the fresco on the Temple of Agriculture painted".

According to what Stirling's data seem to show, Teotihuacan II-III, represented in the Totonacapan and Cotaxtla by Ranchito de las Animas (so closely linked to the culture of the great metropolis) is matched in the Olmec area of Los Tuxtlas by the stratum called Upper Tres Zapotes I, that lies immediately above the pottery belonging to the great La Venta culture.

Consequently we have proposed the name of *Proto-Olmecs* for the authors of more or less related cultures — Teotihuacan II-III, Ranchito de las Animas and Upper Tres Zapotes I — considering Totonaca-Zoqueano groups as their probable founders".

Archeological Olmecs

The origin of the mysterious archeological Olmecs is still a puzzle. Like all the Mesoamericans, they of course came from the north, and ethnically they were certainly of Mongoloid stock.

But how they came to settle in the areas they occupied, from where they began to develop their extraordinary culture and transfer it to other tribes, is something that is not known with complete certainty.

What we do know quite well, however, is the archeogical phenomenon that we call Olmec Culture. We shall look at an analysis of it and at its possible origins.

At the Round Table of the Sociedad Mexicana de Antropología held in Tuxtla Gutiérrez in 1942 to discuss the question of the Archeological Olmecs, the highest authorities expressed various points of view, which can be summarized thus:

1). Caso, Palacios and Covarrubias suggested that it was the most ancient culture in Mesoamerica, mother of the Teotihuacan, Maya, Totonac and others.

2). Covarrubias suggested an early Olmec occupation on the Pacific, particularly in Guerrero, from where it was transferred to the Gulf Coast.

3). Morley, Thompson and MacNeish put forward the theory that there existed a common cultural *substratum* from the Huasteca to the Maya region, and that the *Olmec Culture* arose as a late, minor variation of this.

4). Lastly, Drucker suggested there was a cultural pattern common from Honduras to the Huastec area, and that the *Olmecs* were a series of contemporary specialized cultures within this tradition.

However, everything seems to indicate that the Olmec Culture developed on the Gulf at the moment it modified a widespread ceramic tradition in Mesoamerica. This

Head Stone. Olmeca Culture.
Jalapa, Veracruz.

tradition, that Olmec potters also helped to develop, consisted of flat-bottomed vessels, the use of rocker-stamp decoration, the imprinting of rope and textiles on clay, punching, relief and intaglio, incised or criss-cross designs; stirrup shaped handles, fingernail decoration, zonal decoration, the firing of pottery in reducing atmospheres, black pottery with white edges, etc.

But to repeat, this tradition was widespread in Mesoamerica. What was the Olmecs' contribution to it that made them so different and led them to enjoy a spectacular impetus that turned them into the "mother culture" they have so rightly been called? Their contribution was precisely this: due to the abundance in those regions of the American jaguar *(felis onca)* which they made their totem and center of their religion, (perhaps as a water god) they stylized the feline features of the animal and added them to all their artistic production in clay, stone, and to the small carvings in precious and semi-precious stones that also distinguish the Olmecs as great lapidaries.

But this same ceramic tradition exists from the Panuco River to Central and South America. A comparative study of the Carbon-14 datings given in the places where such pottery has been found, and a discussion of them, can give us the dates of the tradition and help us to reach conclusion as to the chronology of the Olmecs.

Before this, we only wish to say that this pottery developed on sites such as La Venta, so important that it has been suggested that the Olmec culture should more rightly be called the La Venta culture; Tres Zapotes, El Trapiche, San Lorenzo, Viejón, Alvarado, and other sites on the Gulf Coast; but also in Pánuco, Chiapa de Corzo, Mazatlán, Izapa, Ocós and others, and sites in Panama, Ecuador, Peru and the United States. It is on the Gulf where the feline motif is characteristic.

1) Carbon 14 dating for La Venta run from 1154 to 174 B.C. From this it can be inferred that its heyday was

between 800 and 300 B.C., but the dates of its initial development are not known. If this is compared to the *Ajalpan* period of the Tehuacán Caves, where evidence similar to that of Tlatilco and Gualupita, dated at between 1,500 and 1,000 B.C., was found, the beginnings of La Venta can be situated towards 1,500 B.C. at least.

2) At Chiapa de Corzo the first products of this ceramic tradition have, as a date for the middle of its initial period, 1,052 B.C., and so all the Chiapa de Corzo I period is estimated as lasting from 1,300 to 1,000 B.C. For the Cotorra phase of the Santa Martha Cave in Chiapas, which yields the same pottery, there is the date 1,320 B.C.

3) The Ocós phase at La Victoria in Guatemala is very closely related to Chiapa de Corzo I, and is calculated as existing between 1,500 and 800 B.C. This phase shows great similarities to the Chorrera Culture of Ecuador.

4) There used to be dates as early as 2,130 B.C. for the Monagrillo phase in Panama, but now, through comparison of pottery, it is dated of 1,000 B.C. However, the Valdivia Culture of Ecuador has considerably earlier dates: 2,493 and 2,093 B.C., obtained from shells, which has led to the conclusion that it began around 2,500 B.C. This was followed by the Machalilla Culture (2,000 to 1,500 B.C.) and the Chorrera Culture (after 1,500 B.C.), the latter being related to Ocós.

5) The above mentioned pottery was introduced into Peru in the Early Guañupe phase, whose dates are 1,848 and 1,148 B.C., although now 1,200 B.C. is accepted as the most correct. Afterwards follow Cupisnique or Chavín, (after 1,000 or 800 B.C.) and it is this period that shows the greatest similarities to the Olmec culture. After this follows the *Tutchcainyo* complex, dated at around 500 B.C.

6) Lastly, in Pánuco, Veracruz, there is a phase called Pavón, with pottery similar to that of the Olmecs, similarities that become clearer in the following, *Ponce,* phase

that can be dated from 1,200 to 800 B.C.. The Tchefuncte and Hopewell Cultures of the United States, with pottery similar to the Olmec, are dated at between 800 and 400 B.C. The same can be said of Tlatilco, Tlapacoya, Gualupita and other sites that show Olmec influence, and are dated for this epoch at between 1,100 and 800 B.C..

As we have seen, practically all the dates quoted lie between 1,500 and 800 B.C. generally speaking. The only ones that stand out as noticeably different are those of Valdivia in Ecuador. To accept these would mean having to accept that the ceramic tradition we are dealing with originated there, but the dates are very doubtful. They were obtained from shells, the most unreliable organic material when used for chronological measurements by Carbon 14. Moreover, they are dates that agree with neither the Olmec nor with Chavín, as an extremely long period without remains falls between the two.

Perhaps then we would be justified in believing that this pottery developed on the Gulf Coast and from there descended into South America, but in that case, the mystery of its origins would still remain unsolved. The most feasible answer is that the tradition, of Asiatic origins, penetrated North America during the end of the Siberian Neolithic era, between 2,500 and 2,000 B.C., influenced the groups of the north, center and west, and then descended into Mexico. There is, in the east of the United States and at Ajalpan in Tehuacán a tradition of stone bowls, whose shapes were used as a base on which to develop pottery which, because of the malleability of the material, underwent an extraordinarily rapid change until it was free of the stone tradition. It was then that an organized tradition spread from Mexico to Central and South America.

La Venta Culture

The La Venta Culture, which we shall use as an example of the Olmec since we have already said that it is its finest interpretation, apparently began towards 1,500 B.C. if not earlier; Ajalpan between 1,500 and 900 B.C.; Chiapa de Corzo and Cotorra towards 1,400 B.C.; La Victoria in Guatemala (Ocós phase) is linked to Chiapa de Corzo and the Chorrera culture between 1,500 and 800 B.C., in Peru ceramic appears towards 1,200 B.C.; Mesoamerican features enter Peru towards 1,000 B.C. and from there spread to Brazil.

La Venta lies on the low coastal plain of Tabasco, on small elevated areas surrounded by marshes and low-ying hills. This means that it flourished in surroundings suitable for the cultivation of corn, hunting and food-gathering. But one serious disadvantage of the area is that there is no stone. For this reason the inhabitants had to transport great blocks of stone from distant regions on huge rafts or by land to produce their monumental sculptures.

The Olmecs worked andesite, basalt, jade, quartz, diorite, nephrite and other stones obtained by trade, but they also specialized in cutting hard and semiprecious stones, of a bluish-green color, that they transformed into beautiful ornaments and delicate figurines.

Olmec art is distinguished and characterized "by its simplicity and realism in form, by its vigorous and original concepts" but "it is saturated by the feline spirit that is its basic element, and this obsession, dictated by the magico-religious considerations of the tribe, can be observed in all artistic production, both in clay and stone".

At the beginning clay was the most used material. Seated figurines were made with catlike or childlike features, trapezoidal mouths with the upper lip raised, slanting eyes, and squat obese bodies. Sometimes rolls of fat are represented, especially on the so called "Baby face" figurines, that are very realistic.

At La Venta pottery was fired in a reducing atmosphere, by which black, white and gray tones were obtained. There are bowls in pinkish-white, polished white, black with white or red rims, polished black, cream-gray, blackish brown, painted red and other colors; mainly plates and flat-bottomed pots, composite silhouette bowls, ollas and other types of containes. To decorate, cutting, punching, rocker stamps, and geometric and symbolic motifs usually representing the claws and ocellations of jaguar were used.

In the heyday of this culture, the Olmecs specialized in sculpture and bas-relief, mainly in basalt, serpentine and jade. The outstanding achievements in sculpture are the monumental heads, often with feline and Negroid features, "structured and conceived as closed blocks, as a cubic geometrical mass in which the contour is never interrupted".

The perfection of these heads leads one to think of several centuries of experience and improvement.

This monumental art can be observed in other sculptures at La Venta such as *La Abuelita* or Monument 5, with a childlike face and holding a bowl in the hands; or in a sculpture of a seated man-jaguar, now in Villahermosa Museum, with a jaguar-mask face turned up to the sky.

This increase in sculptured art resulted in the pottery becoming coarse at the zenith of the culture, in period III of La Venta. At that time pottery was made in sandy red, reddish cream, sandy cream, rough gray, reddish brown and other colors, that lasted until the Late Classic.

The lack of stone is the reason why the Olmecs have left no monumental architecture. They built round nuclei of mud, with superposed flat stones, treetrunks and straw, all perishable materials that have not survived the centuries.

Finally, as Covarrubias says, these plastic expressions form "the climax of a noble and sensual art, the product of a sophisticated, but sober and dignified esthetic spirit".

"Olmec art is powerful and simple, masterly and original. It is imposing, but free of the complicated symbolism and baroque spirit of the Classic cultures, being closely linked to the formative stages of the basic Mesoamerican cultures, that the earlier they are, the more "Olmec" their spirit".

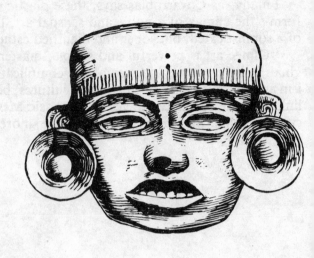

Teotihuacan

Situated northeast of Mexico City and known world-wide, the city of Teotihuacan has, nevertheless, a history still full of mysteries that are the exclusive province of a handful of specialists. A ceremonial and urban center of the greatest importance, the largest in Mesoamerica and one of those that during the Classic period bore most upon other cultures to define themselves and reach the climax of their development, Teotihuacan has been the object of scientific investigations that have led to the partial disentanglement of its past.

It is to be noted that these investigations have not been confined to archeology but, thanks to the Mexican anthropologist Manuel Gamio, propounder of the theory of integrality, have embraced the colonial and contemporary periods so that the vertical development of the Teotihuacan area can be appreciated. But for pre-Hispanic

Mesoamerica, what interests us is the archeological history which unfortunately, unlike the case of other Mesoamerican cultures, we cannot complement with written texts.

In fact, the texts drawn up by both natives and Europeans after the Conquest, hardly refer to Teotihuacan, and as these texts are very late, any reference is completely based on myth. In other words, the texts reflect what the Aztecs said had happened at Teotihuacan at the time of the creation of the gods, principally of the Sun and the Moon. The truth is that for a really scientific approach to Teotihuacan we can count only on archeology and its methods.

However, in order to give archeology more life, we shall try to intermingle the data given by this science with a translation of the Nahua texts gathered from the natives by Fray Bernardino de Sahagún, of the Franciscan Order, that tell of the creation of the gods in Teotihuacan. We shall thus try, as far as possible to synthesize the main information we now have about the magnificent city.

Many centuries ago, perhaps 300 years before Christ, there were two small villages in the Valley where Teotihuacan was to rise later, covering some four square kilometers to the north of the present city. The life there was extremely simple. The inhabitants were mainly growers of corn, squash, chili and beans, but among them however were artisans with advanced techniques in pottery, basketry, stone-working and probably weaving. They possessed a complicated religion, with the god of fire and water deities as their main objects of veneration, as well as complex burial customs. They had perhaps built stone edifices in groups of three, dedicated to their gods.

But... where did the inhabitants of these two small villages come from, who have been calculated to total some 5,000? It is not known for sure, but is probable that they were partly descended from the people that abandoned Cuicuilco, the city with the circular pyramid at the foot of the Ajusco volcano, when the Xitli erupted dramatically and covered the buildings, and whose lava field formed the present Pedregal de San Angel.

It is also probable, though this is still very hypothetical, that another part of the population was of Olmec origin, the mysterious culture that came to life on the Gulf coast that we examined in the preceding chapter.

In time the two villages must have fused to create the Teotihuacan culture, both of them contributing their own cultural traditions.

A group of restless priests and astronomers among them had a flash of genius, and with the religious and astronomical knowledge they had acquired, took the first steps towards the building of the largest, most impressive and most beautiful city in Mesoamerica.

It was with this step that the period known as Proto-Teotihuacano or *Patlachique* ended, that ran from approximately 100 B.C. to the beginning of our era. This gave way to the period known as Tzacualli or Teotihuacan I, which was to last 150 years.

From that moment, news of the existence of the city was gradually communicated to all Mesoamerica, whereupon people began to arrive from distant lands, some on ceremonial visits and some to stay there permanently. It was it this way, for example, that a colony was formed three kilometers to the west of the city consisting of people from Oaxaca, as shown by pottery and the urn found in this area that belong to the Oaxaca periods known as Monte Albán II and IIa, corresponding in time to Teotihuacan I.

By around this time, the population of the city increased to some 30,000 and the metropolis covered some sixteen square kilometers.

What did Teotihuacan people look like at that time? Certainly very similar to what the heads and figurines then made reflect. Some of them are quite elaborate, with rich dress and hairstyles, that most probably repre-

Clay mask. Teotihuacan Culture.

sent priests or sorcerers, the dominant classes. There are also some figures with an extraordinary sense of movement, perhaps representing steps in ceremonial dances.

> *"When it was yet night,*
> *when there was yet no day*
> *when there was yet no light,*
> *they gathered,*
> *they convened, the gods*
> *there in Teotihuacan,*
> *they spoke*
> *they consulted among themselves:*
> *—Come hither, o gods.*
> *Who will take the task upon himself,*
> *who will make himself responsible*
> *for there being day*
> *for there being light?"*[1]

Teotihuacan means "The place where gods are created" or "Place of Apotheosis". The fragment of the beautiful Nahuatl text we translated above confirms the accounts prevalent at the time of the Conquest in the sense that since remote antiquity there had been a tradition that the first gods, the Sun and the Moon, were created at Teotihuacan.

There were two gods who wished to take on the task of ensuring light: *Tecucciztécatl,* "lord of the Snails," powerful and proud, and the humble and poor *Nanahuatzin* "El Bubosillo," an extraordinarily brave god, covered in purulent sores.

> *"And here (in Teotihuacan) there is*
> *what is called the divine brazier*
> *that burned for four years".*

[1] From the Spanish of Miguel León-Portilla

Tecucciztécatl and Nanahuatzin had to throw themselves into the brazier in order to become gods. The purulent god made a sacrifice and then threw himself in without hesitation. The proud Tecucciztécatl lost courage and only fell into the ashes. Hence, Nanahuatzin reappeared in shining glory, as god of the Sun, and Tecucciztécatl with much less light, symbolizing his cowardice, was reborn as the Moon. But neither of them moved; they did not mark the progress of time.

Then the gods asked themselves:

> "How shall we live?
> The Sun does not move.
> How in truth shall we make people live?
> Let the Sun become strong through us,
> Let us sacrifice ourselves, let us all die.

> "There was then death of gods
> There in Teotihuacan.
> And when the sun rose into the sky,
> it was then that the moon
> finally fell into the ashes.
> When it reached the edge of the sky,
> then Papaztac covered its face
> with a rabbit's mask"[2]

Teotihuacan seems to have been planned as a city right from the first period. It centers round a central axis, known variously as the Street, Avenue or Alley of the Dead. This name was given to it by the Aztecs who, when they visited the city for the first time towards the 14th century and saw the mounds already covered by earth and vegetation, did not think they were pyramids once topped by temples, but tombs. And so they called this enormous avenue Miccaotli, or Street of the Dead. The

[2] From the Spanish of Miguel León Portilla

architectural complex lying to the north of the so-called Citadel is also known as the Street (Avenue) of the Dead.

The following years, i.e. from 150 to 250 A.D. known as the Miccaotli or Teotihuacan II phase, mark the greatest extension of the center, which by then covered some 22.5 square kilometers. At the same time the population grew to some 45,000. In this last Preclassic phase, Teotihuacan was on the threshold of its Classic flowering. The city was divided carefully into districts, with religious and public buildings, markets, palaces and multi-family dwellings.

It was then that the typical elements of Teotihuacan the talud and tablero (sloping wall and vertical wall) appeared. But... where did these elements come from? Where they original creations of the Teotihuacan people or were they based on other structures?

East of Mexico City there are some very interesting, very carefully excavated and reconstructed ruins, but unfortunately almost unknown. The name of the place is Tlapacoya, and it was rightly defined by those who excavated it as a transitional Preclassic site. The reason for this definition is that at Tlapacoya the architectonic features of the Preclassic period begin to be abandoned in favor of forms, or rather combinations of forms that were to develop later, during the Classic period. The "talud" (sloping base) was being used together with moldings that afterwards would become the "tablero" (vertical wall).

It was the people of Teotihuacan that took over the development of these elements. When they distributed these features, they made the "talud" smaller than the "tablero" situating the staircase in the center, framed by ramps. In actual fact, archeological excavations and reconstructions give only a vague idea of what the city was like originally, since all the edifices were covered with painted stucco, sometimes in solid colors and sometimes with murals, or else they were covered with relief carvings. Very few remain, due to weathering. It is precisely this

Tlaloc. Mural painting
Tetitla Palace, Teotihuacan.

architecture that leads Teotihuacan to its cultural climax in the Classic period.

Knowledge was being gathered throughout the Preclassic Period: experiments and errors led to the improvement of techniques and the selection of styles. Gods such as Huehuetéotl, the god of fire, who had enjoyed constant veneration, survived in the new period.

The two hundred years before and after the beginning of the Christian era were a period of basic reorientation, not only at Teotihuacn but in other parts of Mesoamerica too. But if vessels and figurines have been interpreted correctly, the Valley of Mexico felt the impact of two different influences. One, that came from the northeast and originated in the River Lerma area, at Chupícuaro, was responsible for a profusion of curious figurines with slanting eyes together with elaborate polychrome pottery decorated with repeated geometric motifs. The second, more significant influence came from the east and included flat-bottomed vessels, pottery with designs in negative painting, the so-called fine orange ware, projecting supports, and perhaps the idea of modeling figurines to represent deities.

In spite of being exposed to new tastes and styles, popular taste inclined towards the old tradition of Cuicuilco-Ticomán, with a few progressive local changes, this, together with the architecture mentioned brought about the beginning of Classic Teotihuacan, towards 300 A.D., a period also called Teotihuacan III or Tlamimilolpa.

By this time Teotihuacan had become the mightiest power in all northern Mesoamerica, and for the next four hundred years its political and religious domination remained unbroken. The Classic years of Teotihuacan witnessed the fulfilment of its founders' dreams.

Once transformed into a real city, with a population estimated of 85,000, Teotihuacan contained special residences for its aristocracy and great dwelling complexes, kinds of communal apartments that are thought to have been inhabited by peasants, artisans and specialists of all types.

Begun in the Preclassic Period, the Avenue of the Dead was by now built, the Pyramid of the Sun was almost finished, and the original Pyramid of the Moon and the Citadel were in process of being raised. After the laying out of the East Avenue, which bisects the Avenue of the Dead immediately north of the Ciudadela, the basic city plan was complete.

Climbing the Pyramid of the Moon that marks the extreme northern limit of the Avenue of the Dead, one is confronted by the great central axis of the city and can marvel at its urban planning. Directly opposite the pyramid is a vast square, flanked by three pyramids on each side. On the right, behind Structure 5, is the sumptuous Palace of Quetzalpapalotl or Quetzal-Mariposa, (Quetzal-Butterfly) with its inner patio surrounded by columns carved with polychrome bas-reliefs, and murals in the inner chambers painted with designs associated with water and the god of rain, whose name at Teotihuacan we do not know but who we will call Tlaloc, the name given to him by the Aztecs.

All this edifice has been perfectly restored. It was perhaps a priests' residence, since after all the priests were nothing less than earthly manifestations of the gods.

Looking again towards the Avenue of the Dead, the eye finally comes to rest beyond the Pyramid of the Sun on the center of the city and the Street of the Dead group, situated where the Avenue of the Dead is crossed by the east-west avenue. This intersection lies half way between the Citadel and the Pyramid of the Sun.

The group consists of stepped mounds, platforms, patios, staircases and possibly dwelling areas all set around a central square. The fact that it is prominently located at the exact center of the principal thoroughfare suggested that it played an important, though as yet undefined, role in the life of the city. Beyond lies the great Citadel, opposite the area that seems to have been the Market, now occupied by shops, restaurants and the Teotihuacan Museum.

It is difficult to distinguish these structures from the Pyramid of the Moon because of the great distance. Both sides of the Avenue are lined by civil and religious buildings. Narrow alleys, like corridors, lead to the residential areas that are mingled with the most important religious edifices.

Anyone who visits the Avenue of the Dead goes up and down numerous staircases, crosses patios that seem to be endless, and has his attention drawn by the talud-tablero combination that is repeated on every platform, sanctuary and altar. This repetition emphasizes the importance of these elements, that are restricted to the religious constructions. But they are not repeated through lack of imagination on the part of the architects, but in order to convey their religious symbolism.

The Citadel is not only an example of the size, precision and extraordinary planning that characterize the apogee of the architecture of Teotihuacan, but also gives us an idea of how the buildings looked in their heyday.

This is an immense structure some 400 meters square, limited by a wide platform on its north, east and south sides. Each one is topped by four small pyramids, with the exception of the east side, that holds three. A wide staircase in the west gives access to the precinct. The platforms enclose a vast courtyard, at the end of which stands the famous Pyramid of Quetzalcóatl. This structure of six superposed terraces with the typical talud-tablero combination, was partly covered by a smooth-faced building, probably after 300 A.D., during the Tlamimilolpa phase.

The facade of this spectacular temple is elaborately decorated with undulating feathered serpents, surrounded by conches and marine motifs. Serpents' heads emerge

*The Pyramids of the Sun and the Moon
as seen from the Pyramid of Quetzalcoatl,
Teotihuacan.*

from a sort of flower with eleven petals, alternating with heads of the rain god with large eye rings, fangs and a kind of bow on the head. There are still remains of red and white paint on this notable stone high relief.

We should try to imagine how impressive the complex must have been in the 4th. century, when the pyramid with six terraces was in its finished state, its carved reliefs emerging from a stuccoed and brilliantly painted facade, and a temple on top illuminated by torches and sacrificial fires. The monotony of the architectonic plan is easily forgotten if one imagines the metropolis flamboyant with color, since from what we can still see, Teotihuacan was a painted city.

This is a most important feature. The palaces around the city were covered with murals: Atetelco, reconstructed so brilliantly by Agustín Villagra Caleti; Tetitla with its orange jaguars, geometric designs, water gods and quetzals; Tepantitla with its procession of priests of the rain god and its "Paradise of Tlaloc" that was a place of eternal joy, games and song where those who died by water went; and other palaces such as Yayahuala, Zacuala, Oztoyohualco, etc.

At this point something extremely important must be mentioned. It was during this period that Teotihuacan's influence extended to other places in Mesoamerica, not only neighboring ones, but even to such remote sites such as Tikal, the Maya city in the Guatemalan Petén. This influence was so sweeping that some anthropologists have been led to wonder whether in fact there was a Teotihuacan Empire. Strange to say, if such an Empire existed, then from that moment to this power has been wielded from the Central Plateau of the present Republic of Mexico. Later the Toltecs and the Aztecs (the latter greatly extending the area) were to occupy with their "empires" the same places that Teotihuacan occupied in the Classic period.

It is true to say, however, that Teotihuacan, like the

Olmecs, was a mother culture. In some cases it was not only this but was also an influence to which other cultures, such as the Zapotec, owe their rise and definition.

Towards 650 B.C. Teotihuacan began to decline, and during the following hundred years the population decreased rapidly. For some unknown reason many people decided to move to the east of the city. This phase is called Metepec or Teotihuacan IV. Spherical ollas' were made but left unpainted, and stamped decoration on pottery makes its first appearance, to become more important in the next and last phase, called Oxtoticpac.

During the end of the Classic Period the manufacture of molded figurines had been important, but no artistic production was enough to prevent or postpone the collapse of the Teotihuacan culture. So ended Teotihuacan, the city of the gods.

"Immediately they began to move,
All began to move:
Young children, old men
Young girls, old women.
Very slowly, little by little they went,
And came to reunite there at Teotihuacan.
There orders were given,
There an elite was established.
Those who became lords
Were the wisemen,
The experts in things occult,
The keepers of tradition".

"Then were established there
The principalities...
And all the people made temples
to the Sun and to the Moon,
afterwards they made many smaller temples".

"There they worshiped,
and there the high priests

of all the people settled.
Hence it was called Teotihuacan,
Because when the lords died
They were buried there..."

"For as they would say:
When we die
We do not really die,
Because we live, we come back to life,
We continue living, we awake,
This makes us happy".

"This is why the aged said:
—whoever has died has become a god.
They said: —There he became a god,
Which means he died".[3]

---

[3] From the Spanish of Miguel León-Portilla.

Tula and the Toltecs

Towards the time of the fall of Teotihuacan, perhaps at the beginning of the 10th century, an important personality appeared on the central high plateau of Mexico, who as Bernal says, is the first "of flesh and blood", meaning that he can be identified and his existence proved. His name was Mixcoatl, and he commanded hordes arriving perhaps from Jalisco or the south of Zacatecas. In time they would be called Toltecs, and although we know nothing about their prehistory, it is reflected mythicaly in a text of Toltec origin known as the "Leyenda de los Soles" (The Legend of the Suns).

However, the history of the Toltecs can be studied in various documents, like the *Anales de Cuauhtitlan* (Annals of Cuauhtitlan) also known as the *Códice Chimalpopoca;* (Chimalpopoca Codex) the *Historia Tolteca-Chichimeca;* fragments of the *Códice Matritsense* and of other pre-

Hispanic texts. All these are of indigenous tradition but there is also a wealth of data in chronicles and histories written by Europeans after the Conquest.

We have already spoken of a very important pre-Hispanic god, Quetzalcóatl. We must distinguish between Quetzalcóatl-god and Quetzalcóatl-man, because there was also a priest whose existence like Mixcoatl's cannot be doubted, in other words also of "flesh and blood". His life and works are not only closely linked with the Toltecs, but he was responsible for their achievements and through him they were to succeed in revolutionizing pre-Hispanic ideas, since Quetzalcóatl-man was a great metaphysical thinker, a mystic.

Mixcoatl conquered the Valley of Mexico and some neighboring regions and harassed the remnants of the Teotihuacan culture but did not, as was believed before, *destroy* Teotihuacan: only vestiges, more than decadent, survived of Teotihuacan, so Mixcoatl only destroyed the few remnants of the old splendor.

Mixcoatl then built the first Toltec capital, Culhuacan. The reader is reminded that this city together with its founders the Culhuas, a Toltec branch, have been referred to in the section on the historical Olmecs. It is interesting to note that Culhuacan continued to exist until the arrival of the Aztecs three centuries later. It was then the only surviving Toltec city, and continued to be inhabited until the Conquest and even up to the present day, forming part of modern Mexico City.

Mixcoatl added Morelos, Toluca and Teotlalpan to his domains, but in his forays, something very important happened to him according to Sahagún, who relates that he met a woman who was not Toltec, since:

"...the woman Chimalman went out to meet him, and laid on the ground her shield, threw down her arrows and stood naked before him without skirt or blouse. On seeing her Mixcoatl shot his arrows at her: the first he shot simply passed over her and she only bent her head; the second he shot passed by her side and she bent the shaft; the third he shot, she simply caught in her hand; and the fourth he shot she extracted from between her legs. Having shot at her four times, Mixcoatl turned and went away. The woman immediately fled to hide herself in the cave of the great ravine. Again Mixcoatl came to fit himself out and provide himself with arrows; and again he went to look for her, but saw no-one. He then abused the women of Cuernavaca. And the women of Cuernavaca said: "Let us seek her". They went to fetch her and said to her: "Mixcoatl is looking for you; because of you Mixcoatl abuses your younger sisters" ...Yet again went Mixcoatl and again she went out to meet him; she was as before standing and covering her pudenda; as before she laid her shield and arrows on the ground. Again Mixcoatl shot at her repeatedly without result... After this, he took her, he lay with the woman who was Chimalman, who soon afterwards found herself with child...".

During Chimalman's pregnancy Mixcoatl was assassinated by one of his captains, so she went into refuge with her parents at Tepoztlán in the present State of Morelos, from where they came originally. There the son of Mixcoatl was born posthumously: Ce Acatl Topiltzin Quetzalcóatl, and his mother died in childbirth.

The reason for his name is that Quetzalcóatl was born in a year Ce Acatl (one Reed) according to the native calendar, and all children were named according to the day on which they were born. This year, according to the native calendar, could be 843, 845, or 947 A.D., and as the *Chimalpopoca Codex* says that he died in a year of the same name (Ce Acatl), he lived for 53 years. But this we do not know for certain. What we do know is that Quetzalcóatl had prophesied his return in another year One Reed, and by extraordinary coincidence Cortes reached the coast of Mesoamerica in one of these years. This made Moctezuma Xocoyotzin, who governed the Aztecs at that time, think that he was Quetzalcóatl returning to claim the throne he was keeping for him.

Topiltzin means "Our Prince", and Quetzálcoatl "Precious" or "Plumed Serpent". Our Prince One Reed Plumed Serpent was brought up by his grandparents in Tepoztlán, culturally linked to the Xochicalco we have mentioned, which may be geographical Tamoanchan. In both cities Quetzalcóatl-god was worshiped, and this is why the main pyramid at Xochicalco is decorated with huge feathered serpents. Topiltzin was educated within this cult and took the name of his god.

Some time later Quetzalcóatl was called to the throne of Culhuacan, that since the assassination had been occupied by the usurpers. Tradition says that Quetzalcóatl agreed, returned to the Valley of Mexico, found the remains of his father, whom he deified and buried on the Cerro de la Estrella, where he built a temple to him. He conquered the usurper and towards 980 A.D. decided to settle at Tula. Some historians have supposed that Quetzalcóatl founded this capital, but the *Chimalpopoca Codex* states that he went first to Tollanzinco (today Tulancingo in the State of Hidalgo) where he arrived in a year 12 Acatl, which could have been 870, 922 or 974 A.D. According to this Codex, Quetzalcóatl mounted the throne of Tula after Huetzin, which proves that Tula already existed since it had had lords before, in the year 3 Acatl, i.e. 873, 925, or 977 (the date now most generally accepted by historians for Quetzalcóatl's arrival in Tula is 980).

Finally, the *Codex* speaks of his expulsion from Tula as occurring again in a year 1 Acatl, which could be 895, 947 or 999 A.D. It is interesting that all the important events of Quetzalcóatl's life (and, as we have seen, also his death) occurred in years of Reed.

The great difficulty in distinguishing between Quetzalcóatl god and man is due to the fact that the texts transmitted by Sahagún's native informants confuse the two personalities, the mythical with the historical, as is

Lead-colored vessel inlaid mother of pearl.
Toltec Culture.

shown by the following texts dealing with the houses Quetzalcóatl caused to be built at Tula:

"There was also a temple that was of his priest called Quetzalcóatl, much more polished and beautiful that his own houses and which had four chambers: one lay toward the east and was of gold, and it was called the golden-faced chamber, because in place of whitening it had cleverly nailed plates of gold; and another chamber lay toward the west, and this was called the emerald and turquoise chamber because within it had fine work of all manner of precious stones, all laid together in place of whitewash as a mosaic that was marvelous to behold; and another chamber lay toward the south, called South, which was of divers marine shells and in place of whitewash had silver, and the shells which filled the walls were so subtley placed that no joints were visible between them; and the fourth chamber lay toward the north, and this chamber was of red stone and richly decorated with jasper and shells".

"There was also another house of featherwork, which inside had feathers instead of whitewash, and this had four more chambers; and one lay to the east and this was of rich yellow feathers in place of whitewash and was of all manner of yellow feathers and extremely fine; and the chamber in the west was called the chamber of plumage, that had in place of whitewash all classes of the richest feathers, the feathers of a fine blue bird and which were laid and stuck on cloths and nets covering the inner walls most cleverly in the manner of tapestry, whence it was called quetzacalli, that is chamber of rich feathers; and another chamber that lay to the south was called the house of the white feather because all within was of white feathers, in the manner of crests and had all species of rich white feather; and the other chamber was in the north and was called the chamber of red feathers, the inner walls being covered with all manner of feathers of precious birds. Apart from these houses they made others, most curious and of great value".

In addition to appreciating the rich description of the text and the splendor of such marvelous (and certainly mythical) constructions it is important to notice that the four houses were orientated towards the four directions of the universe, and that each direction had a color according to the Toltec concept: red in the north, white in the south, yellow in the west and blue (or green, the colors of the turquoise) to the west.

Another text that refers to Quetzalcóatl and perhaps reflects the "Golden Age" of the Toltecs better than any other, says:

"And they also say that the city was very rich and had all that was requisite and necessary to eat and drink, and that corn was most abundant, and the gourds very fat, an armspan round, and the ears of corn were so big that they were carried between two arms; and the stems of amaranth were very tall and fat and that people climbed them as if they were trees; and that they sowed and harvested cotton of all colors, that were red and yellow and flesh-colored, and purple, whitish, green and blue and dark brown and gray and orange and tawny and these colors of the cotton were natural, thus it grew; and they also affirm that in the said town of Tula dwelt many and different species of bird with rich plumage of various colors, and other birds that sang sweetly and softly. And also the said Quetzalcóatl possessed all the riches in the world, of gold and silver and green stones and other precious things and there was an abundance of cacao trees of many varieties. And the said subjects of the said Quetzalcóatl were very rich and wanted for nothing, nor was there hunger or lack of corn, and they did not eat the small ears but with them heated the baths as if with wood".

But this extraordinary life was bound to come to an end. The native texts perhaps relate in a mythical or

98 — DEMETRIO SODI M.

symbolic way what happened historically. Groups living near the Toltecs who could not, or did not wish to absorb their culture, worshipers of bloodthirsty gods, principally *Tezcatlipoca,* decided to attack the Toltecs, who according to the next of Sahagún's native informants:

> *Were careful in religious matters*
> *only one god did they have,*
> *they held him to be the only god,*
> *they invoked him*
> *they appealed to him,*
> *his name was Quetzalcóatl.*
> *The guardian of their god,*
> *their priest,*
> *his name also was Quetzalcóatl.*
> *And they were so respectful in religious affairs,*
> *that all that the priest Quetzalcóatl ordered them,*
> *they carried out faithfully, they did not distort.*
> *He would say to them, would impress upon them:*
> *—"This only god,*
> *Quetzalcóatl is his name,*
> *Demands nothing*
> *but serpents, buttlerflies,*
> *that you must offer up to him,*
> *that you must sacrifice to him".*[1]

Thus Quetzalcóatl the metaphysical thinker shows himself to us as he makes known to the Toltecs an only god, perhaps a dual one, as is shown in another very beautiful native text, which says of Quetzalcóatl:

> *He prayed, to his god, to something*
> *in the inner reaches of the sky*
> *to her with the petticoat of stars, to him*
> *who makes things shine;*
> *lady of our flesh, lord of our flesh;*

[1] From the Spanish of Miguel León-Portilla.

"Atlantes" of Tula, Hidalgo.
Toltec Culture.

she that is dressed in black, he that is dressed in red
she who gives ground to (or supports) the earth,
he who covers it with cotton.
And towards the other world he directed his cries,
it was known,
towards the place of Duality (Omeyocan)
the place of the nine hazards
of which the sky is composed. [2]

As can be seen, the god of Quetzalcóatl is being referred to here in both sexes indiscriminately, and his place is said to be *Omeyocan* or place of duality. The priests of Tezcatlipoca were not satisfied with offerings of mere serpents or butterflies, they wanted human sacrifice. Again legend and history unite. His enemies, through magic, try to bring about Quetzalcóatl's fall until, to finish, they used a mirror and "gave him his body".

This already very old man who had dedicated his life to teaching and meditation came face to face with his own old age, with the terrible results of time. He could not refrain from expressing his distress, and the magicians took advantage of this by offering him a remedy. They made him drunk on pulque, which led Quetzalcóatl to sleep with his sister, Quetzalpétlatl, and to fail in all that he himself had tried to instill into the Toltecs.

Immediately afterwards (towards 999 A.D.) Quetzalcóatl fled (or was expelled, according to some sources) and made his way to *Tlillan Tlapallan* (the region of the red and the black, i.e. of wisdom) which in all probability was Yucatan. This is how the native historians would explain the Toltec in the northern Maya area, (which we shall study later) as well as the arrival of *Kukulcán* in that region, a leader whose name is the same as Quetzalcóatl (Kukulcán means Feathered Serpent in Maya)

2
From the Spanish of Miguel León-Portilla.

But Quetzalcóatl did not go alone, or directly, to Yucatán. First he wandered through the central valleys and settled for a time at Cholula, where he was highly venerated. He finally reached the Gulf Coast. An indigenous text tells us of his pilgrimage in company with his faithful disciples.

> *And thus they (the Toltecs) believed*
> *in their high priest Quetzalcóatl,*
> *And thus they were obedient,*
> *and given to the affairs of god*
> *and most fearful of god,*
> *whom all obeyed,*
> *all believed in Quetzalcóatl*
> *when he abandoned Tula...*
>
> *And so much did they trust in Quetzalcóatl*
> *that they all went with him, they entrusted to him*
> *their wives, their children, their sick.*
> *They arose, they began to move*
> *the old men, the old women,*
> *no one failed to obey,*
> *they all began to move.*
> *At once he went out into the sea*
> *Towards the red-colored land,*
> *there he disappeared,*
> *he, our lord Quetzalcóatl.*

Two myths, or perhaps two versions of one myth, refer to what happened on the Gulf Coast. According to the first, Quetzalcóatl simply built a raft of snakes, embarked and became lost out to sea on his voyage to *Tlillan Tlapallan,* the land of wisdom.

According to the second (which we personally prefer) Quetzalcóatl built a huge funeral pyre on the beach, into which he threw himself and then from it rose many beautiful birds, the different manifestations of his spirit, and he became *Tlahuizcalpantecuhtli,* Lord of the Dawn House, Venus as the morning star. From being in anguish at the passing of time he becomes a star and so rules time.

Archaeological Tula

Both sources and archeology tell us that Tula was governed by a dynasty of ten persons, and here we transcribe the table that according to the *Chimalpopoca Codex* contains eight of the governors of the city. We shall give the native dates of events and also the three possible corresponding dates in our calendar, as we did for the doubtful dates of Quetzalcóatl. So, No. 1 shows the list of native dates, No. 2 the date according to the synchronization shown in the Codex, but as there can be an error of 52 or 104 years (one or two pre-Hispanic cycles) on the part of those who transcribed the hieroglyphic text into written text, line 3 gives the date allowing for an error of 52 years, and line 4, allowing for 104 years.

Tula, as we have seen, was founded at the beginning of the 10th century, and excavations have shown that it was destroyed by fire towards the end of the 12th or beginning of the 13th century. The Toltecs then moved to the Valley of Mexico and the Sierra Nevada (Cholula) but some certainly went to northern Yucatan, Guatemala and even to San Salvador and Nicaragua whose descendants, the Pipil Nicarao (Pipiles) not only spoke Nahuatl but continued to worship Quetzalcóatl, which was verified in 1538 by Father Francisco de Bobadilla.

Tula in the State of Hidalgo is certainly the Tula of Quetzalcóatl-man, but now we come up against the myth that caused a difficult problem of archeological interpretation; we shall conclude the chapter with an attempt to elucidate it.

The plumed serpent or serpent-bird combination appeared in Mesoamerican cultures as early as the Preclassic

THE HISTORY OF TULA ACCORDING TO THE CHIMALPOPOCA CODEX.

| 1 | 2 | 3 | 4 | |
| | | 52 | 104 | |
YEAR	YEAR	YEAR	YEAR	MOST IMPORTANT EVENTS IN THE HISTORY OF TULA.
1 Tochtli	726	778	830	Beginning of the Toltecs. Their year-count begins.
1 Tecpatl	752	804	856	Mixcoamazatzin inaugurates the Toltec empire.
1 Calli	817	869	921	Mixcoamazatzin dies; Huetzin ascends throne.
1 Acatl	843	895	947	Topiltzin Quetzalcóatl born.
12 Acatl	870	922	974	Topiltzin Quetzalcóatl arrives at Tollanzinco.
3 Acatl	873	925	977	Topiltzin Quetzalcóatl rules Tula.
1 Acatl	895	947	999	Topiltzin Quetzalcóatl expelled from Tula; Matlacxóchitl ascends throne.
10 Tochtli	930	982	1084	Matlacxóchitl dies; Nauhyotzin ascends throne.
12 Calli	946	998	1050	Nauhyotzin dies; Matlaccoatzin ascends throne.
1 Calli	973	1025	1077	Matlaccoatzin dies; Tlicohuatzin ascends throne.
9 Tochtli	994	1046	1098	Tlicohuatzin dies; Huemac ascends throne.
6 Calli	1918	1070	1122	Human sacrifice begins; 7 years' famine.
13 Acatl	1063	1115	1167	War begins.
1 Tecpatl	1064	1116	1168	Toltecs disperse.
7 Tochtli	1070	1122	1174	Huémac commits suicide at Chapultepec.

era, but everything seems to point to this combination being related to aquatic deities. How far is this relationship preserved in subsequent epochs? This we do not know; we may even go so far as to think that after the Preclassic the combination becomes more of an abstract concept, with no specific relationship to anything.

However, at Teotihuacan, in the so-called Pyramid of Quetzalcóatl in the immense enclosure of the Citadel, the plumed serpent appears in all its splendor, carved in stone and alternating in fact with representations of the god of water.

Is this a reminiscence from the Preclassic? This we do not know either, but we believe two things: first, that in the case of Teotihuacan the spiritual concept of the plumed serpent is already separated from the aquatic divinity but continues in close relationship; second, everything seems to indicate that the idea of a supreme deity, Quetzalcóatl, crystallizes in Teotihuacan.

But something happened after the fall of Teotihuacan and the arrival of Mixcóatl with his hordes who then began to receive the name of Toltecs. Indigenous texts tell us:

First they arrived there
at the place called Tollantzinco *(Tulancingo, Hidalgo)*
and straightway they moved to Xicocotitlan,
The Toltecs were victorious
at all times
until they approached
Chichimec territories.
The memory is now lost
of how long they wandered.
They came from within the plains,
between the rocks.
There they saw seven caves,
and made of them their temples,
their places of worship.

*Stela depicting
Quetzalcoatl.
Xochicalco, Morelos.*

106 — DEMETRIO SODI M.

*And these Toltecs
were always most advanced*[3]

What we have seen is reaffirmed by this text, that the Toltecs founded Tula and settled there after the ruin of Teotihuacan, carrying on the great tradition of Náhuatl culture that is certain to have originated in Teotihuacan. The confusion that has existed in reference to these two cities, aggravated mainly by native and European texts written after the Conquest, a confusion that still persists to some extent, may perhaps be explained and solved with these final considerations.

Toltécatl is a Nahuatl term meaning "artist", and *Toltecayotl* another that means "Toltechood" or "union of arts and artists". In the Toltecayotl lived the *Tlacuilo* or painter, who possessed black and red earth, the *zuquichiuhqui* or potter "who taught clay to lie", the *amantecatl* or featherwork artist, and also all kinds of artisans, builders, sculptors, etc., who all, as the texts say "put their divinely inspired heart into their works" (Tlayoltehuiani).

This is why, before the grandeur and artistic richness of Teotihuacan, this city was believed to be the Toltec capital. However, when systematic archeological excavations were begun at Tula Xicocotitlan in the State of Hidalgo, everything indicated that this city was the real Toltec capital. It was then that the confusion began. How could such a city, relatively small and poor in comparison to Teotihuacan be the origin of the Toltecayotl, of the marvelous world of the arts?

The answer certainly lies in a simple play of ideas and words. The Toltecs of Tula, still semi-savages at the time of the fall of Teotihuacan, absorbed the remains of its unmatched cultural grandeur, Teotihuacan being certainly the capital of the *Toltecayotl,* of the union of arts and artists since they rightly deserved the title of Toltecs, artists.

[3] From the Spanish of Miguel León-Portilla.

But those from Tula, although in many aspects they could not improve on their masters at Teotihuacan, were also great artists and can in their own right be called Toltecs likewise. This, moreover, is the name of their ethnic affilation as vouchsafed by both history and custom.

There is a native text in which the Aztecs describe the impression they received on first visiting Tula during their long period of wandering as they came from the north. This text, it will be seen, perhaps makes the Aztecs the first archeologists of the continent:

> There were many things in Tula,
> There the Toltecs buried many things.
> But this is not the only trace
> of the Toltecs that can be seen there.
> Also their pyramids, their mounds,
> There at the place known as Tula Xicocotitlan.
> On all sides they can be seen,
> On all sides can be seen remains of clay jars,
> of their bowls, of their figures,
> of their dolls, of their figurines,
> of their bracelets,
> on all sides are their vestiges,
> in truth they were living there
> together, the Toltecs.
> The Toltecs were skilled people.
> It is said they were artists in feathers,
> practiced in the art of applying them.
> From ancient times they possessed this art,
> it was in truth their invention,
> the art of feather mosaic.
> Hence, from ancient times they were entrusted
> with shields, insignia,
> those that are called apanecáyotl.
> This was their heritage,
> thanks to which were granted insignia.

They made them things of marvelous beauty
attached the feathers
the artists knew how to place them,
in truth they put in them
a divinely inspired heart.
What they made was marvelous,
gorgeous, worthy of admiration.

These Toltecs, it was said,
were Nahuas,
were not Popolocas,
though they were also called
the ancient inhabitants...
They were rich,
For their skill
soon brought them wealth.
Hence, it is now said
of he who quickly becomes wealthy:
"He is a son of Quetzalcóatl
and Quetzalcóatl is his lord".
So was the existence and life
of the Toltecs.[4]

Once again our story comes a full circle with Quetzalcóatl.

---

[4] From the Spanish of Miguel León-Portilla.

Oaxaca
and the Gulf Coast

Despite the fact that this chapter will be a very brief synthesis, we did not wish to exclude the region of Oaxaca and the Gulf Coast cultures from our rapid study of Mesoamerica, even though in the case of the latter we shall simply list the culture traits.

The ancient history of Oaxaca is very closely linked to the archeological zone of Monte Albán, one of the most impressive in the superarea. For this reason, its name is always associated with the chronological periods of Oaxacan archeology, which are the following (after Piña Chán):

The Olmec peopling of Oaxaca
    Monte Albán I
(Upper Preclassic: 800 to 300 B.C.)

The Birth of the Zapotec tradition
    Monte Albán II

(Protoclassic period: 300 B.C. to 100 A.D.)

The height of the Zapotec tradition
Monte Albán IIIa and IIIb

(Postclassic period: 100 A.D. to 800 A.D.)

Decadence of the Zapotec tradition
Monte Albán IV and V

(Postclassic period: 800 to 1521 A.D.)

The Valley of Oaxaca was the cradle of a group of civilizations that were developed at various times by peoples that generally speaking, we still do not know. Mitla, Zaachila and above all Monte Albán, all lying in the neighborhood of the present State Capital (the City of Oaxaca) offer us a reasonably comprehensive chronology of the cultures that expanded in the Valley up to the time of the Conquest. Monte Albán was occupied perhaps from the 8th or 7th century B.C. onward by pre-Zapotecs, groups equivalent to those of the Valley of Mexico cultures of the Upper Preclassic. These initiated sculpture and architecture, and everything seems to point to their being groups of archeological Olmecs.

During the Monte Albán II period a culture began to develop that was to result in the Zapotec civilization, thanks to the arrival of new peoples, perhaps originating in Chiapas and Guatemala and who mixed with the Olmecs, the first settlers. The Zapotec civilization can be recognized thanks to the influence from Teotihuacan that arrived at the end of Monte Albán II and overlaid the Olmec and Mayance traditions of the groups already there.

The phase probably lasted from the 4th to the 7th century A.D., and from the Valley of Oaxaca the Zapotec culture spread to all the surrounding regions.

Zapotec urn.
Monte Albán, Oaxaca.

This is followed by Monte Albán IV, which was a period of decadence for the Zapotec civilization. The pressure brought to bear by newly arrived peoples, the Mixtecs, resulted in the progressive abandoning of Monte Albán, while on the other hand Mitla grew in importance. It cannot be stated firmly however whether this city was inhabited by predominantly Mixtec peoples or by Zapotecs who had been subject to strong Mixtec influence.

Towards 1400, in the last phase of Monte Albán (V), the ancient Zapotec capital became an immense necropolis, which does not mean however that tombs had not been built there earlier, but that Mixtec Chiefs had themselves buried in the holy city in old Zapotec tombs. Burials were carried out with ostentation, proved by the treasure of tomb VII, one of the richest archeological treasures of the world.

The two enemy nations, Zapotecs and Mixtecs, fought desperately for the control of the central valleys of Oaxaca. The result was that the Zapotecs became fewer and fewer until they were reduced to the mountainous regions in the northeast of the state and the Tehuantepec Isthmus. In addition, war encouraged the appearance of a military class and fresh outbreaks of human sacrifice.

Towards the second half of the 15th century and the beginning of the 16th, Zapotecs and Mixtecs united to defend themselves against the Aztecs. Moctezuma I (1440-1469), Axayácatl (1469-1481) and Ahuítzotl (1486-1502) waged wars of conquest from which the Mixtecs were first to suffer. It appears that during the reign of Moctezuma I a military colony was established in the Valley of Oaxaca, and an expeditionary group was sent to conquer the Isthmus. They were not immediately successful, and in fact had to lay siege to the Zapotecs for four years before returning in triumph to the Valley of Mexico.

When the Spanish arrived, Oaxaca was governed by two representatives of the Aztec *Tlatoani*, the *Tlacochtecuhtli* or commander of the garrison, and the *Tlacatecuhtli*

Vessel. Mixtec Culture.
Zaachila, Oaxaca.

responsible for the administration of the region. In 1521 Oaxaca was conquered by the Spanish under Diego de Ordaz, who founded the old city of Antequera, today the city of Oaxaca, but at that time simply a fortified post.

Pre-Hispanic Ethnography of the Gulf Coast

The total area of the Gulf Coast can be divided into three: the Huastec region, along the Atlantic slope; the Totonac region, running from the Río Cazones to the Río de la Antigua, and the Southern Veracruz region, from Cotaxtla to Coatzacoalcos. The gap between the Huastec and Totonac areas corresponds to a *Nahuat* "wedge", that of Nautla. It must be noted that information for this region is very unequal. The data for the Huastec region, although scarce and brief are of great interest; sources relating to the Totonacs are richer, especially concerning religion. As for the southern part (Nahua, Olmeca-Uixtotin-Mixtec, Popoluca and Mixe) information is so poor that only a few isolated culture traits can be mentioned.

Thus, according to 16th century sources, and after Kirchhoff, the culture traits would be for the *Coast dwellers*:

Tattooing; shaven head; filed teeth; purposely blackened teeth; noseplugs of various shapes; beards as an attribute; an 18-month year; flying-pole game (Volador); confession of sexual transgressions (to the goddess *Tlazotéotl*, to jaguars, etc.) the Quetzalcóatl complex; mutilation of the male member (circumcision, autosacrifice, etc.); ritual use of rubber.

Stone ceremonial axe.
Gulf Coast Culture, Veracruz.

Coast and Isthmus dwellers

Copper axes; human heads or the skin of the face as trophies; use of the *quechquémitl;* sodomy as an institution; 5 as a ritual number.

Features common to all the Coast

Importance of fishing; importance of weaving arts (textiles decorated with feathers); crown-shaped hairstyles braided with feathers; elliptical houses (according to Melgarejo).

Features of the Huastec area

Terms of family relationship according to the Omaha system; bases for houses; round houses; burials in houses; houses occupied by ten persons on average; nudity (absence of the maxtlatl); sashes (the only article of clothing for men); maxtlatl in two pieces; men with very long braided hair; painted hair (red, yellow and other colors); blue body-painting; very large perforation of the septum; nose plugs of feather quills; filed teeth; pectorals and ear plugs of engraved shell; caps; maces as shown in the codices; war trophies; scalps or any hairy part of the enemy's body worn round the neck as a trophy; inebriation by pulque enemas; great importance of shamanism and sorcery; hypnotism; cauterizing with fire (torches); healing with mirrors; piercing the tongue with fishbones; absence of the temazcal (steam bath); the universal god named Paya (Feathered little Bowl); the Huasteca as the birthplace of the gods Tlazoltéotl-Ixcuina, Quetzalcóatl, Xipe and Mixcóatl; decorative motifs of clouds.

"Nichos" Piramid. Gulf Culture.
Tajín, Veracruz.

Totonac features

Extraordinary agricultural richness; transplanted, not sown, corn; pottery made with leaves; globular clay jars as beehives; shaven heads; *quechquemitl;* netting; clothing different from the southern Nahuas; *xicolli;* long habits (priests); tortoiseshell shields; a divine trinity; the Sun *(chichim,* "he who kills"); divine corn-earth complex (Cintéotl-Tlazolteótl?); morning star (Quetzalcóatl?); flying pole game; communion with a cake of blood, rubber and seeds; young goddess who seduces young men in the tianguis (market) and afterwards kills them; absence of *Tzompantli* or place for the skulls of sacrificial victims (the Spanish saw the first one at Ixtacmaxtitlan, a Totonac and Mexican town); the temples take care of the poor; priests chosen by the people; conches on priestly vestments; newlyweds spend days in abstinence and fasting; yoke-ax-palm archeological complex; "padlocks" of carved stone.

Southern Veracruz

Veneration of caves (Tepeyólotl?); bipartite government.

Olmeca-Uixtotin-Mixtec

Great variety of costume; rubber sandals.

Coatzacoalcos

Suits of bark (others of cotton); cannibalism; "they would kill a great number of Indians (prisoners) in the afternoon near the river, and wash their entrails therein, on which they dined''. Painala, only daughter of the lord, inherits the domain.

Chinantla

Liana bridges; 5-meter-long spears; small shields; musical bow; fruit wines; tripartite government with one head.

Many of these ethnographic features of the Gulf Coast peoples exist even today.

The west of Mesoamerica

The area comprising the West of Mexico is in fact formed of various modern states: Sinaloa, Nayarit, Jalisco, Colima, Michoacán and part of Guanajuato and Guerrero.

In this wide area cultures flourished that were more or less similar, those of Guerrero being the only exception. However, archeological information on the West of Mesoamerica is unfortunately still scarce, since it remains the least explored zone. In this chapter we shall deal mainly with the Tarascans, that is to say with the archeology and history of the best known and studied group of all the West, that lived mainly in the present state of Michoacán.

The Preclassic in Michoacán:

While cultures constantly appeared and disappeared in Mesoamerica, as has been described, the West, perhaps due to its isolation, kept its own local developments. This, in the long run, was what saved it from Aztec domination as they were never able to conquer most of the area, particularly in the case of the Tarascans, who were never defeated.

Thus, the Preclassic art of Michoacán is different from that of other peoples, but is nonetheless of high quality, especially in regard to pottery and representations of the human figure.

The two best known archeological sites dating from this period are El Opeño (Michoacán) and Chupícuaro (Guanajuato). At El Opeño, to date the most ancient site discovered in the West of Mexico, there are several tombs hewn out of the white rock, with a domed chamber high enough for human remains to be deposited inside. They are entered down three or four steps, also hewn out of the rock, and are on average 1.50 meters deep.

Clay figurines decorated with "pastillage" (clay appliqué), similar to types D and C of the Middle Preclassic of the Valley of Mexico were found in them. In addition there were projectile points with concave bases, jadeite ear ornaments, a small idol in serpentine with Olmecoid features, effigy vessels, jade beads, vessels with negative painting, etc. showing that the group that inhabited El Opeño had a highly developed culture.

However, the most important site in the West is without a doubt Chupícuaro, which belongs to the Upper Preclassic. This archeological zone is very large but very spread out, consisting of a series of low hills lying along the River Lerma and its tributaries. The inhabitants of Chupícuaro, in order to escape the flooding of these rivers, deposited their dead and placed their cemeteries at the top of these hills. The hill of El Rayo, between the River Lerma and its tributary El Tigre or Coroneo is the most thoroughly investigated. Almost 400 human burials were explored and 46 dog skeletons and an ossuary found. It is curious to observe that offerings appeared together with skeletons reclining on their backs, while those lying face down were unaccompanied, perhaps as a sign of their inferior status or of their being prisoners. Offerings were projectile points of obsidian, metates (grinding slabs) and manos (rollers); clay figurines, bone and clay earplugs, ornaments of shell, necklaces, bone and stone tools, ocarinas, flutes and wide variety of vessels.

The people of Chupícuaro were certainly sedentary and already were beginning to build platforms covered with stone and floors of baked mud for the bases of their huts. Their grew corn, beans and squash, and ground the corn on stone metates; the presence of some mortars indicates the use of chile and perhaps tomato. They also practiced food-gathering, hunting and fishing.

In Apatzingán, Michoacán, some culture traits show that Preclassic groups survived: three-legged earthenware bowls of composite silhouette and sometimes human faces like those of Chupícuaro; three-legged vessels with wide incised decoration and perforations reminiscent of the Galupita (Morelos) styles; flattened figurines in the tradition of Guanajuato; vessels with negative painting or decoration done a fresco, etc. This means that the Preclassic lasted longer in Michoacán than in other parts of Mesoamerica.

The Tarascans

The history and development of the Tarascan culture has gradually been clarified. For a long time, anything found in the West of Mexico was simply described as "Tarascan" but we now know the distribution and chronology of this culture much better. The Tarascan Culture belongs entirely to the historical horizon, making it much easier to piece together its historical and cultural panorama, since historians and chroniclers left much information. For example, thanks to them and to the excavations at

Clay figurine. Western Culture.
Colima.

Ihuatzio, Michoacán, we know that toward the 10th and 11th centuries there was Toltec influence at work among the Tarascans. This is evident from a Toltec style Chacmool and a type of coyote in stone that was perhaps a throne in the shape of the wild animal, both pieces being typical products of the Toltec Culture.

The Lienzo de Jucutácato also attributes the introduction of copper working among the Tarascans to certain Toltec immigrants. According to the Lienzo these immigrants settled near deposits of copper in the valley of the River Balsas, on the southern limits of Michoacán.

The name "Tarasco" is really a late and erroneous name given to this group by the Spanish, who were called "tarasco" by the natives when they married their daughters, "tarasco" meaning son-in-law. Their more correct name is *Poré* or *Purépecha*.

Archeology shows that central Michoacán has the features of a uniform culture. It is here that "yácatas," stepped pyramids combining a circular and a rectangular mass are found. Stone was used to form the nucleus of the constructions, but sculpture and carving in stone are rare. They were built on a single platform. As for pottery we find ollas with stirrup handles, mouths and spouts; bowls with supports in the form of spirals, rattles or human figures; boot-shaped vessels with vertical handles and wide mouths; cooking pots and vessels in the shape of pumpkins; double, three-legged bowls; toys and miniature vessels. Negative painting and finely burnished black pottery predominate.

Clay pipes are also common, either with circular, flattened, or spiral stems; work in jade is rare, but the articles in obsidian (ear- and lip-plugs) and rock crystal are extraordinary, as is the work in gold, silver and copper, either cast by the lost wax process, or the copper plated with gold. Post-burial cremation was practiced. Bone musical instruments have been found.

Clay figurine. Western Culture.
Nayarit.

Many of the elements appear in places such as Ihuatzio, Tzintzuntzan, Jacona, Quiroga, Pátzcuaro, Tangancícuaro, Huétamo, etc., and Tarascan influence can be seen in Guanajuato, Querétaro, Guerrero, Colima, Jalisco, Nayarit and part of Sinaloa.

Toward the end of the 14th century, King Tariácuri formed an alliance of three cities with a view to structuring the Tarascan groups into a kind of Empire. These three cities were Tzintzuntzan, Pátzcuaro and Ihuatzio, Tzintzuntzan being the most important, and the capital of the Tarascan alliance, especially after the death of Hiqugaje, governor of Pátzcuaro.

Tariácuri's successor Tangajoan extended the kingdom notably, and was followed by Zuanga and Tzitzic Pandácuare, also known as Characu or Crown Prince, who died in 1479. He forced the kingdoms of Zacatollán, Colima, Zapotlán, Jalisco and Tonalá to submit to him. Tzitzic Pandácuare fought the Matlazinca in 1462 and in 1479, at Tajimaroa repulsed an Aztec invasion. During the reign of his son Zuanga (the second king of this name; 1479-1519) the Spanish arrived in Mesomerica and the king died of smallpox, brought by one of the negro slaves belonging to Pánfilo de Narváez. The last Tarascan king was Tangajoan, also known as Caltzontzin, who was forced to abdicate. Thus ended the ancient history of the Purépecha people.

The Mayas

Within the context of Mesoamerica the Mayas developed a culture that might be called "privileged". Many writers have been led to consider this culture the most important in Mesoamerica because of its notable achievements in the fields of arithmetic, astronomy, chronology and art, regarding the latter as those showing the greatest refinement and perfection. But the truth is that even if this is correct, the Mayas do not escape from the common cultural substratum to which we referred earlier, since in all their cultural manifestations, even in the most deeply intellectual, we find the unmistakable imprint of Mesoamerica.

The culture developed in a vast territory of some 325,000 square kilometers corresponding in general terms to the present States of Yucatán, Quintana Roo, Tabasco, the eastern half of Chiapas in Mexico; the greater part of Guatemala (except the Pacific coastal fringe); Belize (ex British Honduras); and a narrow zone of the eastern part of Honduras and El Salvador. In this immense region there are great variations of climate, vegetation, and mountain systems, in short, different ecosystems that were hosts to the Mayas from remote eras.

Basically the territory can be divided into three natural zones containing these ecosystems. One consists of mountain chains interspersed with tablelands, the Cordillera of Central America, forming a semicircle in the southwest, south and southeast. Another is formed by the inner basin of the Department of the Petén in Guatemala, with the adjacent valleys that originate in the surrounding hills, including the Yucatán peninsula. The third area is the north of the same peninsula, flat, low-lying, extensive, limestone, covered with bushes and scrub.

The Mayas were actually made up of various groups with approximately the same ethnic affiliation, and therefore with more or less similar physical characteristics. They spoke various languages all of a common linguistic stock (in the Maya area some 24 Mayance languages are still spoken today) and were heirs of one same culture, which did however have variations according to the region.

Among the main surviving Mayance languages, the following stand out in importance: Chol, Chontal, Tzeltzal, Tzotzil, Jacatelco, Mam, Quiché, Cakchiquel, Kekchí, Mopán, Lacandón and the Maya proper of Yucatán, which with others are grouped into families making up the great Maya linguistic stock. One of the Mayance languages, Huastec, is now spoken in a region in northern Veracruz, a remote region which Maya speakers somehow reached when they migrated from Maya territory before the culture had really defined itself. This happened perhaps some 1,200 years B.C.

The Huastecs were not the only to migrate, but on the other hand they were the only ones to leave what was later to be the Maya area of settlement. Movements of other

Maya speakers also occurred in remote epochs, according to claims based on linguistic studies, but these groups stayed within the territory. In other words, "they began to find a comfortable position for themselves". Linguistic studies put forward the theory that a proto-Maya community existed some 2,500 years B.C. in an area that might be the present site of Huehuetenango in Guatemala. The members of this community spoke the same language, proto-Maya, which gradually split up, and the speakers of these various dialects were obliged to migrate. These defined the Maya area, with the exception of the Huastecs who as we have seen moved much farther.

As for the chronology of the Maya culture, it follows by and large the general chronology of Mesoamerica, but with perhaps more clearly marked divisions between the different periods, for several reasons. Before examining these reasons however, we wish to point out something important.

The pre-Hispanic patterns of settlement were more or less the same throughout the superarea. That is to say that there were ceremonial centers that for many years archeologists insisted had not been permanently inhabited except perhaps (and this in order to explain the existence of obvious living areas within the precincts) by priests, temporarily, when they were carrying out certain long ceremonies. Modern archeology has proved that priests and nobles lived permanently around the ceremonial centers, in palaces that often actually intruded on the ceremonial area.

For many years archeologists have dedicated themselves to the exploration and study of these "ceremonial centers". Thanks to them we know the ceremonial patterns of settlement and those of the ruling classes quite well. But little is known about the ordinary people, such as the peasants who supported those in power with their tributes. Mainly within the Maya region, archeology has directed its most recent efforts towards the discovery of these settlement patterns, and this new focus of attention has revealed information that revolutionizes Maya chronology.

Excavations have recently been in process in the zone called Cuello in the north of Belize (practically in the Petén) that have produced dates for Maya remains associated with wood (measurable by the Carbon 14 method) of between 2,450 and 2,750 years B.C. or 26 centuries before our era and so, one thousand years earlier than what up to now was considered to be the beginning of Maya civilization.

This does not only cause difficulties of chronological adjustment, but also historical problems. For a long time the Olmec civilization has been considered a "mother culture", and mainly as the mother culture from which the Maya civilization absorbed the necessary bases for its later development. But if, according to what the archeologist Norman Hammond discovered in Cuello, the Maya civilization existed almost a thousand years before the Olmecs, history complicates itself and much research will be necessary before it can be readjusted. Hammond himself points this out when he says:

"In effect one season of work at Cuello had pushed back the antiquity of the Maya by a full millennium and the prehistory of the lowlands by more than 1,600 years. Moreover, the establishment of such an early date for the possible inception of the Maya Formative period had effectively removed the Olmec civilization from further consideration as the initial stimulus of Maya culture and even suggested the possibility that Maya culture acted as an influence on the emergent Olmec society".

But let us go back. Before Cuello caused these problems, we said that we had perhaps more exact divisions between the different periods, due to various reasons. There are two main ones. The first is that, thanks to intensive excavations in the Maya region, there exist numerous and often complete ceramic sequences that of course are invaluable, using stratigraphy in dating ancient cultures; this, together with many series of Carbon-14 datings. The second, highly important reason is that with spectacular and extremely detailed studies of Maya inscriptions it has been possible to interpret almost all the chronological hieroglyphs used by the Mayas to record periods of time, and correlate them first with the Julian and then with the Gregorian calendars, with such a measure of exactness that even the equivalent of months and days can be calculated. In this there are two systems of correlations: A, due to Herbert J. Spinden that pushes back 260 years the dates given by system B, which we owe to the collaboration of three specialists whose name it bears, Goodman-Martínez-Thompson. The latter is the most widely accepted as it has proved to agree more with other existing systems of dating.

As the Mayas dated stelae, paintings and even pottery with this system, the reading of chronological hieroglyphs gives us the exact dates of many historical events and of material remains of various types. This can be understood better knowing that hieroglyphs representing place names as well as personal names, birth, coronation and death of the main historical personages in several Maya cities have now been identified. We can trace, a little roughly but more or less satisfactorily the historical events and the occurrence of specific historical periods of cities like Tikal in Guatemala.

So, to summarize, traditional Maya Chronology, can be divided into the following periods according to Eric J. S. Thompson who until his death was probably the greatest expert on the Maya.

132 of 176 — DEMETRIO SODI M.

Formative Period

From ca. 500 B.C. to 325 A.D.

This period is approximately equivalent to the one that in other parts of Mesoamerica is known as the Upper Preclassic and the beginnings of the Classic. This was a period of cultural dependence, inasmuch as although clearly defined Maya characteristics already appear, specially in the great numbers of figurines with perfectly rendered Maya ethnic features, the civilization had not yet succeeded in freeing itself completely from the influences of its neighbors, principally the Olmecs. The pottery of this period, in various styles, is called Mamom and Chicanel.

Classic Period

This lasts from 325 to 925 A.D., but is subdivided into three: Early Classic, from 325 to 625; Flowering from 625 to 800 A.D., and Decline from 800 to 925 A.D.. It has been possible to make such exact divisions with the help of the above mentioned calendrical correlations, among other things. The pottery types of the Classic period are called Tzakol and Tepeu.

During the Early Classic the typical features of the Mayas emerge, namely temple constructions using the corbeled arch, and the cult of time, shown by the incredibly precise record of its progress on stelae carved with large numbers of hieroglyphs, not only chronological but also "literary", or to do with writing. External influences completely disappeared at this time.

During the Flowering everything reached its climax. Architecture, carving, painting, pottery, minor arts, principally gem cutting, astronomy, arithmetic, hieroglypic writing, etc., all developed to their greatest splendor. While the preceding period was confined mainly to the Highlands of the Maya area, the Flowering took place in the Lowlands, and the Highlands suffered a marked decline.

Lastly, in the Decline, perhaps the influence of alien groups slowly corroded the Maya civilization to such an extent that at the end of this period and in the following extremely brief one, called by Thompson the Interregnum that lasted some 50 years, the glory of the Flowering descends to levels as low as those of the Formative epoch.

For us the history of the Maya civilization proper ends here, but the descendents of the Classic Mayas, inheritors of what was mainly a peasant culture, still underwent other historical processes. After the Interregnum follows the:

Mexican Period

From 975 to 1200 A.D. During this period the Maya civilization suffered influences and invasions by peoples from the Central Plateau, Toltec in culture and Náhuatl in speech. What archeology reveals would explain, to some extent, the myth that refers to Quetzalcóatl's departure towards the "Land of Black and Red", i.e. Wisdom, from the Gulf of Mexico on a raft made of snakes. According to the Mayas themselves, the Toltecs then reached the Yucatan peninsula, led by Kukulcán, a Maya word meaning the same as the Náhuatl Quetzalcóatl: Feathered Serpent.

Finally, during the:

Period of Mexica Absorption

Between 1200 and 1540 A.D. various alliances were formed between towns governed by Maya families and by families of Náhuatl or Mexica origins. The last of these, the league formed by the cities of Uxmal, Chichén Itzá and Mayapán marked the complete decline of the Maya culture when it ended in a bloody war. The result was that when the Spaniards arrived they found a poor, divided territory that was only a shadow of its ancient grandeur.

As it is impossible to deal with all aspects of the Maya civilization here, we have been forced to pick out only three. We hope that in examining these more closely they will produce enough information to enrich the stark historical data presented with the chronology. These aspects are: Writing and Chronology, the Life of the Maya Woman during the Classic period (a wholly original subject, we believe) and Maya Architecture, at least its most noteworthy achievements, in relationship with other plastic arts.

Writing and Chronology

Until a short time ago it was commonly said that Maya writing not only had not been interpreted or deciphered, but that it would never be possible to read it. Nowadays this is only partly true. We believe that is in fact true that Maya hieroglyphs will never be "read", but at the same time, that it will be possible to interpret large tracts. Great progress has been made in this field thanks to the collaboration of various specialists, particularly E.J.S. Thompson, Tatiana Proskouriakoff, Heinrich Berlin, Yuri Knorosov, David H. Kelley and many other modern investigators, basing their research on old glyph interpretations and identifications by such men as the picturesque abbé Brasseur de Bourbourg. He is said to have become a priest simply to be able to come to America as a missionary and fulfill his childhood dream: to know the ruins of Mesoamerica.

Among the contributions of Brasseur is that of having discovered the most important European chronicle on the

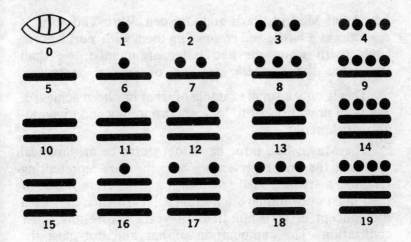

*Maya numbers from 0 to 19
with the bar and dot system.*

Maya civilization: the *"Relación de las Cosas de Yucatán"*, written by Diego de Landa, a Franciscan who was also Archbishop of the peninsula. In this book Landa reproduces what he calls a Maya "alphabet", copying the hieroglyphs drawn by his informants and giving them what he believed to be their phonetic equivalents. From then it became the rage among specialists in ancient writing to decipher the Maya system on the assumption that it was phonetic. At the beginning of this century they had to relinquish their efforts since they had made scarcely any progress in half a century. It was then that investigation was concentrated on the mathematical and chronological hieroglyphs, with the spectacular progress already mentioned.

Gradually efforts were made again with texts, and appreciable results have been obtained. It has been possible to read complete sentences phonetically, and to interpret whole sections of the only three remaining Maya Códices, which are named after the cities where they are now kept: Madrid, Paris and Dresden. With Thompson's readings as a basis, and comparing them with Yuri Knorosov's (with whom he had bitter arguments), we shall transcribe the phonetic reading of several sentences.

This is only a small example of what has been achieved. We shall now proceed to look at chronology and unavoidably arithmetic.

The Mayas had three basic ideograms or arithmetical symbols; the dot, representing one; the bar, representing five and a stylized shell representing zero. Here is one of their most outstanding intellectual achievements: they used the concept of zero hundreds of years before any other civilization. The combination of bar and dot gave the arithmetical sequence from 1 to 19 only, since their arithmetics was based on a vigesimal system. In other words, just as we can only represent 0 to 9 in each of the positions of our numerical succession which is decimal, the Mayas could only represent from 0 to 19.

Zero was a shell. One, was one dot; two, two dots; three, three dots; four, four dots, and five, a bar. Six was formed by a bar with one dot above; ten by two bars, one above the other; eleven was two bars and one dot and so successively up to nineteen, which was three bars and four dots. Instead of counting digits horizontally, the Mayas counted vertically bottom to top. Thus, in the first position, the lower, they recorded the units, in the second the twenties, in the third the four-hundreds, in the fourth the eight-thousands, and in the fifth the sixteen-thousands, i.e. multiples of 20 just as our positions denote multiples of 10.

In this way the dot, that is one, means 20 in the second position, but in order to write 20 it is necessary to draw a zero below to signify that the dot is in the second position and therefore is worth 20. A dot in each of the five vertical positions we have mentioned would mean 168,421. What marvelous simplicity, that requires only one ideogram, the

READINGS OF GROUPS OF GLYPHS ACCORDING TO THOMPSON AND KNOROSOV

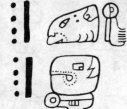 **Bolon yocte** - name of a deity (according to Thompson)

  Kintun yaabil u cuch - drought is its burden (according to Thompson)

  **Yaxhaabil kintunyaabil** - drought for the new year (according to Thompson)

 Buluc - eleven (according to Knorosov)

 Tzul - dog (according to Knorosov)

 Cutz - turkey (according to Knorosov)

 Kuk - quetzal bird (according to Knorosov)

 Kuch - vulture (according to Knorosov)

U poc ti chaan Can Moo Kintun - fire of the macaw in heaven: drought (according to Knorosov)

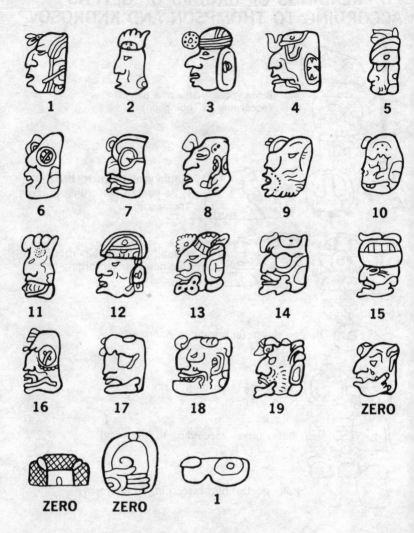

Variations on the heads of Maya numbers. The emaciated jaw of number 10 is repeated through until 19 together with the repetition of the heads from 1 to 9.

dot, to represent such a high number for which we need five different ones.

Like all the Mesoamericans the Mayas had two calendars, which however they combined and counted simultaneously. There was the solar calendar of a fraction over 365 days, the most perfect ever invented by man, and a ritual calendar of 260 days. These were combined by a simple permutation, as the common denominator of both is five. However, to be able to fit the calendars into the numerical system, they had to make a modification. They continued to represent units in the first position, which in this case became the unit of time, i.e. the day, called *kin*. In the second position, the twenties that were comparable to one month, as the second Maya unit of time consisted of 20 days and was called *Uinal*. But, from the second to the third position, instead of multipiying 20 x 20 to obtain 400, they multiplied 20 x 18, resulting in 360 days, a unit of time they called *Tun,* an incomplete year since 5 and a fraction days were missing. This error was corrected by additional calculations that were also recorded on the chronological stelae of the Classic period, on which the system we are describing, known by the name of "Initial Series", was used.

Afterwards, 20 became the multiplier again, but in the fourth position another unit of time of 7,200 days (and not 8,000) is obtained, called *K'atun* or 20 *Tunes,* and in the fifth, a period of 144,000 days called *Bak'tun* or *Tunes.* The Mayas divided time into 18 months of 20 days each (18 x 20 = 360) plus one month of five days (18 x 20 + 5 = 365), and every day and every month had its own name. For the ritual calendar the names of the days were the same, but they were not counted by months but by sets of 13. So the days were counted in order from 1 to 13, and day 14 was prefixed by a number 1, so that at the end of the first "set", day 20 was preefixed by a number 7. When the second "set" began the first day, instead of being prefixed by the number one (as in the first count)

INTRODUCTORY GYLPH

INITIAL SERIES
TZOLKIN DATE: 13 Ahau

SUPPLEMENTARY SERIES
HAAB DATE: 18 Cumku

Stele E. de Quiriguá: the introductory glyph, the initial series and the sumplementary series. The date indicated is 9.17.0.0.0. 13 Ahau, 8 Cumku which Sylvanus Morley interprets as approximatley 771 A.D. This is the largest known Maya stele, measuring 10.5 in height and weighing about 65 tons.

was prefixed by the number 8. This was repeated successively until number 1 again prefixed the first day. This gives 260 different combinations of number and day names.

Both calendars give a great number of combinations of numbers, days and months that in turn produced a myriad of deities, all intimately related to time. This made Eric J. S. Thompson say that no people has ever glorified, considered and worshiped time as much as the Mayas. Time was god. Anxious about the march of time, they solved their problem very simply, they deified it.

But of course, the Mayas had to begin to count time from a definite date, otherwise they would not have been able to record its passage. This "anchor point" within the combinations mentioned was a date 4 Ahau 8 Cumkú, 4 Ahau being the date according to the ritual calendar, and 8 Cumkú that of the solar calendar. We have purposely not yet given the names of the two calendar systems because in actual fact they are not known. However, experts call the ritual calendar *Tzolk'in* and the solar *Haab*. According to correlation B, the anchor point in time, necessarily mythical, is equivalent to 3113 B.C., from which date time was counted. So a period in time or some historical event, was recorded something like this: since 4 Ahau 8 Cumkú have elapsed so many *Bak' tunes,* so many *K'atunes,* so many *Tunes,* so many *Tunes,* so many *Uinales,* so many *K'ins* and we have arrived at such and such a date in the Tzolk'in. The moon was in this position and has passed through another, and we have reached, at the same time, this date in the *Haab*.

Afterwards the necessary corrections were made in the inscription and the dates and positions of other planets were given, all this being mixed with "literary" writing. But an illustration like the one accompanying this text, tells much more than a thousand words.

In short, the Mayas not only developed the most perfect calendar ever created by man, they were also the first to use an ''anchor date'' for their computations, to give a relative value to the numbers according to their position, and to use the concept of zero. As we said earlier, an intellectual achievement for man to be proud of, for at least in these aspects the Mesoamericans too distinguished themselves in their contribution to universal culture.

The Maya woman during the Classic Period

We have seen how during the Formative Period there began a figurine cult, and among these the representation of woman was very important. Like the Preclassic figurines in other areas of Mesoamerica, those of the Maya Formative perhaps show woman as a female deity, or as the incarnation of some concept important to them, perhaps closely linked to fertility, as is the case in Tlatilco on the Central Plateau.

Although in the following period, the Classic, covering some 600 years, the representation of woman grows richer as it is transferred to carving, painting and even pottery, there are almost as many problems in defining her role as in the Formative, but our information, ethnographically speaking, increases. Let us look at three examples.

The ruins of Tikal, Palenque and Bonampak belong to the Classic period. Recently Peter Spier and Alice J. Hall reconstructed with text and illustrations the social and economic life of Tikal, as far as it was possible, with the help of archeological explorations. In this, they refer to such different aspects as building methods, how stelae were carved, how the markets functioned, and the daily life of the inhabitants of the region. In the two last aspects, the presence and activity of woman was of great importance.

"The Castle" from *"The Warriors Temple"*. Chichen-Itzá, Yucatán.

We see the noble family resting before the midday meal. Various women are moving about in the house, but they are not all noblewomen. We know that there was a rigid class system among the Mayas, and so the woman in the magnificent illustration who is placing her baby on cotton cushions and sheets that soften the bench where she herself is sitting, is the only noblewoman of the group. In front of her an old woman, the child's nurse, observes the scene while other women pour drinking water and take corn from containers to make "atole" (gruel). Results of female activity can be seen everywhere in this scientific reconstruction. Pottery making was the business of the women. They chose suitable clay, softened it with water and mixed it with ground shell or quartz, then molded the container. Religious pottery, that for offerings or commemorative purposes may have been made by experts under the vigilance of the priests, but then just as nowadays, domestic pottery was doubtlessly the business of the women. Even now it is easy to see the Maya Indian women of Campeche or the Altos de Guatemala producing beautiful pottery with techniques and shapes that are thousands of years old.

Weaving was also a feminine occupation. The wife wove and embroidered clothes for her husband and children and if the family was rich, she had slaves to help her weave lengths of cloth as a tribute to the local chief. The Dictionary of Motul is rich in terms that give us information on the Maya woman, including for example:

Ix Mol

> "Supplier, Indian
> woman who supplies the
> others when they weave and
> spin the work of one among
> many; she circulates
> among all to collect chocolate
> for all to drink"

*Detail of a mural painting
to be seen in room No. 2. Bonampak, Chiapas
Copy by A. Villagra.*

This casual commentary conjures up the picture of a group of women who, while weaving beautiful designs on strap looms, exchange news and drink foaming chocolate from gourds.

And the products of this very work decorates the house of the nobleman of Tikal.

The life of the peasant, who fed the nobles and priests with his tribute, was quite different. But his life was more peaceful perhaps, as he trusted in his gods and in the conjurations of his priests as he worked intensely.

Another illustration in the same work shows a mother kneeling before her "metate" (quern) grinding nuts gathered from the cashew tree into a paste that she will bake into cakes tasting of chestnut. One of her daughters is weaving cotton cloth with a complicated design, while another, carrying her child in her "rebozo" (shawl) peddles fruit. The neighbour, in a very nearby house, is preparing some of the vegetables that her husband and sons have grown on raised terraces in the forest behind the houses. Everywhere there are baskets, "ollas" (spherical containers), pots, examples of female labor, and the most important products of this society: sons. Some are playing with a spider monkey and a coati, their pets. Another, very small and naked, is climbing up to where his mother is preparing the vegetables, and inside the house another woman is breast feeding her small son.

In this idyllic picture we discover the role of woman and her activities which have been preserved up to the present day among the Mayas: wife, mother, teacher and a very important element in economic life as potter, weaver of cloth and baskets, the person in charge of preparing the food that she herself partly obtains, and her husband's collaborator in preparing agricultural surplus for sale in the market, where she is often the one to sell it.

In the 16th century Diego de Landa wrote his book *"Relación de las Cosas de Yucatán"*. The descriptions we have just read are based on concrete remains found at Tikal during scientific exploration. It is impressive to find that Landa's texts, which refer to the Maya woman of the 16th century and not to the woman of the by then remote Classical period, describe her as carrying out the same tasks and duties, and living in a similar way.

Faced with a shortage of space, I shall quote rapidly and literally a very free selection of some of Landa's paragraphs. It will be easy to realize how rich the information about woman is in his book:

"The Indian women brought up their children under the harshest and barest possible conditions. They were allowed to go naked until the age of 4 or 5, when they were given a small blanket to sleep on and some strips of cloth with which to cover their modesty, like their fathers, and the girls were covered from the waist downward. The women gave breast much because they never stopped, as long as they were able to give their children milk although they might be three of four years old, whence there were many strong ones among them".

"The Indian women of Yucatán are usually better proportioned than Spanish women, and bigger and better made, but not so broad in the loins negresses... They do not paint their faces as in our country... but consider this licentiousness. They have the custom of filing their teeth with certain stones and water".

"They pierced their noses... to place there... a piece of amber and considered this very elegant. They pierced their ears to wear earrings... They painted their bodies from the waist upward — except the breasts when feeding... They bathed very often in cold water... (and) also, bathed in hot water".

"They used to apply to their bodies... a certain red ointment... They anointed themselves with a certain ...fragrant sticky gum... Which I believe to be liquidamber... and after this they were elegant and sweet-smelling".

"They wore their hair very long and formed it into a very sophisticated style, in two parts, and they braided it for another hairstyle".

To terminate the description of the Maya woman's appearance, (given the conservative nature of the culture) I will finish with a quotation from Father Baeza dealing with dress, that perhaps was similar to that worn by the woman of the Classic period, as far as carvings seem to indicate:

"The women clothe themselves with... white cotton cloth, and their dress is simply a skirt to the ankles and a "huipil" (long overblouse), wide and square with narrow openings for the arms that are covered down to the elbows and this overblouse falls over the skirt to a hands-pan of the hem: they cover their heads and part of their cheeks and arms with a headdress likewise of cotton, and go barefoot except for one or two...".

Now let us look at Bonampak, whose murals also give us information on women. Among the magnificent representations of human beings in these paintings that were reconstructed and described by Agustín Villagra, there are on the upper part of the east wall: "Three women seated on a stone throne painted green and decorated with red circles" engaged in various actions. "The first, an old woman, is delicately and elegantly eating something she has taken out of the container beside her, while a fat, paunchy servant kneels before her waiting to deliver something he has in his hands, apparently thorns. The second seated woman is chatting to one standing behind the throne, while the third talks to the nursemaid sitting opposite with a child in her arms. Their dress (although they are certainly noblewomen) is very simple; the light tunics are simply decorated with a green border; they are wearing simple necklaces, bracelets and ear ornaments; their hair is bound with white ribbons. The old woman

Female clay figurine.
Maya Culture. Jaina, Campeche.

covers her little remaining hair with a turban''... in short, there is nothing new under the sun.

The third example, Palenque, is much more dramatic. When Dr. Alberto Ruz discovered the famous tomb in the Temple of Inscriptions, he found a container beside the door where the remains of six or perhaps seven people had been deposited, among them remains of females and children. Does this represent the mass sacrifice of a family, that of the person in the tomb perhaps, as an offering or as company?

It seems very probable: Eros and Tanatos. And so woman's life cycle completes itself: the beloved companion of man during life becomes his companion in death on his journey to the underworld.

Maya Architecture

Maya architecture has its beginnings in the Formative Period although, as we have seen, civilization at that time had not yet been able to free itself from external influences. A monument discovered at Uaxactún, a few kilometers north of the vast city of Tikal, belongs to this era. The edifice is known as E-VII Sub, in the E. section of the city. This gives us an idea of the complexity of Maya settlements. The plan drawn up by archeologists is divided into sections and edifice VII in section E was covered by another after some years. As this part is more recent, it was in a very poor state of preservation, so the archeologist decided to remove it and leave uncovered the older building: the "sub".

This is a construction standing on superposed terraces, with a stairway on each side, all framed by ramps decorated with masks representing the jaguar, possibly as the rain god, and in a completely Olmec style. All the mound was originally covered with beautifully polished stucco, and on the upper part stood a temple which, being built of perishable materials disappeared, but not without leaving traces of its supports. On the upper part were found the holes where the posts supporting the temple had originally been placed, and with this evidence it was possible to reconstruct its ground plan. As this is the same as that of a hut, we can deduce that from that time until now, Maya huts have remained practically the same.

We have said that it is in the Classic Period that the characteristic element of Maya architecture appears: the corbeled arch. There are complementary features too, moldings, columns and roof combs that, together with superposed terraces, are combined to give us the different styles of Maya architecture. The main ones, and their characteristics are the following:

Petén Style

Characterized by edifices rising in stepped terraces, with a sloping ("talud") main mass and salient corners; staircases that project from the facade of the buildings sometimes decorated with stuccoed masks. There is more solid masonry than spaces which means that the walls are very thick and the chambers very narrow; very high roof combs supported on the rear wall of the temples, facades with stucco decoration, etc. Cities such as Uaxactún, Tikal, Piedras Negras, Nakum and Calakmul are built in this style.

Palenque Style

Vertical bases; stairways bordered by ramps; temples with two chambers or corridors, the latter being the sanctuary, roof combs placed above the central wall; facades with friezes running parallel to the vaults and decorated with stuccoed figures; more empty space than solid masonry, etc. The cities of Palenque, Toniná, Copán, Quiriguá, Yaxchilán, Bonampak and Lacanjá belong to this style.

Rio Bec Style

Characterized by the decoration of the constructions, consisting of stylized pyramidal bases with figured stairways, built like tall ornamental towers; stone mosaic, as in Xpuhil, Rio Bec and Hormiguero.

Chenes Style

This contributes to the Puuc style, and both are related to the Rio Bec. Sloping, stepped bases, spaces divided by columns, vertical friezes, roof combs at the front, and very elaborate decoration in which elements such as representation of houses, panels of Greek Key patterns, lattice-work, small column drums, colonettes, large masks of the rain god, all in mosaic of perfectly cut and assembled stone, are features. Cities in Campeche and Yucatán such as Hochob, Edzná, Xcalumkín, Sayil, Labná, Chacmultún and Uxmal are of this style.

Mexica Style

This style is largely a result of the Toltec influence in the northern Maya region, but nevertheless has many features reminiscent of the Puuc style. Bases and platforms with high sloping and vertical (talud and tablero) faces or cornices predominate; stairways with heads of snakes where their ramps begin; altars decorated with skulls; serpent columns, etc. To this style belong the cities of

Chichén Itzá, Tulum, Mayapán, Cobá, Acanceh and late cities in Yucatán and Quintana Roo.

Sculpture and painting were closely linked to architecture, and sculpture both in the round and in bas relief is perhaps the most notable single feature of Maya art. Stucco, stone and wood were used; stelae, altars, vertical faces, lintels, jambs, columns, stairs, etc., were carved. There are examples of sculpture in the round such as atlantes, chacmols, (statues of a deity of Toltec origin) and human figures, but high and low relief carving is much more common.

Painting was decorative but also had a religious and historical meaning. It was used mainly in frescoes on walls in connection with architecture, but also appeared in codices, on pottery, stucco, columns and facades, showing mythological or religous scenes as well as realistic, descriptive or narrative ones such as scenes of war, landscapes, animals and customs.

Pre-Hispanic Maya civilization came to an end in 1540 when T'Hó fell into the hands of Francisco Montejo, the Conquistador who would found the city of Mérida on the same site, present capital of Yucatan and first Captaincy General of the Peninsula. But the Maya of Itzá lineage, who had taken refuge on the lake of Petén, where they founded their last capital, Tayasal, which did not fall until 1695, preserve to date the ancient Maya culture.

Let us finish with a text from a Maya book of Colonial times, the *Chilam Balam of Chumayel*, whose symbolic contents would seem to prophesy the end of the Maya civilization:

> *The moon, the wind, the year, the day;*
> *all march on, but also pass on.*
> *All blood reaches its resting place*
> *just as all power reaches its throne.*

The Aztecs

Sahagun's native informants communicated to him a myth about the birth of Huitzilopochtli, their principal deity, god of the sun and of war, the divinity that led them to supremacy in Mesoamerica during the 15th and the beginning of the 16th centuries.

The myth tells that a woman called Coatlicue (literally, "she of the skirt of serpents"), who was charged with keeping clean a temple on the Cerro de Coatepec, near Tula, was sweeping the building when she saw a beautiful ball of feathers drop from the sky, and put it away in her bosom. When she had finished her work, and tried to find the feather ball, it was no longer there, it had disappeared. At that same moment she became pregnant, although she had been a widow for many years.

When her principal daughter, *Coyolxauhqui,* who was the moon learnt that her mother was pregnant, she regarded it as an insult and spoke to her brothers, the Centzon Huitznahua or Four-hundred (innumerable) Southerners, the stars, and persuaded them to go and kill their mother to avenge themselves for the dishonor she had brought on them. Coatlicue became very sad and hid in the temple to wait for her sons, and with them, death. But one of them, *Cuauhuitlicac* betrayed them and went to tell his mother everything they were doing and from where they were approaching the miraculous fruit of Coatlicue's womb, who was none other but Huitzilopochtli. He gave Cuahuitlicac instructions and induced him to continue bringing information.

When Coyolxauhqui and the Southerners finally reached the hilltop where the temple stood, Huitzilopochtli was born at the same moment, and put on his warrior's dress, his *apanecúyotl,* and one of his helpers lit a serpent of firebrands called Xiuhcóatl. Using this as a sword, Huitzilopochtli cut off the head of Coyolxauhqui, which rolled down the slopes of the cerro (hill) of the serpent, or Coatepec; he also dismembered her. He also set of in pursuit of her brothers the Southerners, who fled, and he did not rest until he had killed them and put on their war insignia. This was how he saved his mother and also became the Sun and the god of war. But this is not the only meaning of the myth. It also symbolizes the eternal march of time, in the following way. Coatlicue, apart from her other attributes, is goddess of the earth. Every morning she gives birth to Huitzilopochtli, the sun, brought into the sky by the Xiuhcóatl, or fire serpents. At this moment he defeats the moon and stars, his sisters, and reigns triumphant during the day. At nightfall he covers himself with his *nahual* (a kind of double or disguise) and wanders through the underworld, until the earth gives birth to him again. The Aztecs, so rightly called "The People of the Sun" by Alfonso Caso, named themselves the chosen people whose mission it was to ensure that the Sun survived. As the Sun was also the god of war and needed to be fed with human blood to keep alive, the

Aztecs became a warlike and bloodthirsty people, that practiced human sacrifice on a grand scale.

But this is the myth. It appears that Huitzilopochtli, also known as Mexi, really did exist and was one of the first Aztec chief, who later diefied him. This was perhaps after he defeated Coyolxauhqui and the Southerners, which could be the mythical explanation of real feats of war between different ethnic groups, those that the Aztecs had to face during their long pilgrimage from their place of origin to the Valley of Mexico. As the Aztecs came from the north the tribes they fought were necessarily southerners. At all events, the myth reflects what León-Portilla has called a mystico-bellicose vision of the Universe.

Curiously enough, some of the *Tlamatinime* or Nahua wisemen of the Aztec period kept alive the tradition of the mystic thinking of Quetzalcóatl at the same time as this belief. The Aztecs were the direct heirs of the ancient beliefs that originated in Teotihuacan, source of the Náhuatl culture, which they received by way of the Toltecs. Nevertheless, in the times of the Aztec governor or *Tlatoani* Itzcóatl, this way of thinking was changed, with the help of such radical measures as burning the Codices which preserved Quetzalcóatl's beliefs, into a mystico-bellicose vision. This is why there are so many completely divergent texts among those that native informants transmitted to Spanish historians, particularly Fray Bernardino de Sahagún, which show clearly the two tendencies.

There is a post-Cortesian Codex called the *Tira de Peregrinación* or *Boturini Codex*. In it the Aztecs recorded, with dates, places and events, all that happened to them during their long migration from their more or less mythical place of origin to their settlement at México-Tenochtitlan. Their place of origin was called *Aztlán* or Place of Herons, and from this toponym comes the tribal name *Azteca*. On the first leaf of the Codex appear the first Aztecs coming from an island, crossing the waters of what is apparently a lake. Jiménez Moreno says that there was a mythical place called Aztlán situated on the island of Mexcaltitlán, possibly the one illustrated in the Codex. This island lies in a lagoon on the coast of Nayarit, where there is still a place called Aztlán.

Kirchhoff points out that many years before leaving the mythical Aztlán, the tribe led a nomadic life, and that the legend speaks of another place of origin called Chicomoztoc, The Seven Caves, or The Womb, that was in Culhuacan, or place of the Culhuas. This has already been localized near Yuriria in the State of Guanajuato. The fact is that the Aztecs originated certainly from the present State of Guanajuato, from some place in a quadrangle formed by Salamanca, Celaya, Salvatierra and Yuriria.

The dates and the elucidation of facts is a difficult and obscure problem from their leaving Aztlán until they arrived at Tula. From Tula up to the foundation of their capital, México-Tenochtitlan, the route, dates and events are clear and known well. Perhaps the Aztecs were the last in a series of nomadic groups, among which they must also have been included before, that roamed the north of Mexico and for reasons yet unknown found themselves obliged to emigrate southward.

According to the Aztecs, they were always led by Huitzilopochtli, which means "Humming-bird of the Left", and who appears right from the first leaf of the Codex. An indigenous text about the migration says that Huitzilopochtli addressed the Aztecs with:

"*I shall go before you as a guide,*
I shall show you the way.

Straightway the Aztecs began to come
hither, they live, they are painted,
the places through which the Mexicas passed
are named in the Aztec tongue.
And when the Mexicas came,

truly they were wandering without a course,
they were the last to come.

When they came
as they were making their way,
they were not received in any place.
On all hands they were censured.

No one knew their faces.
Everywhere people said to them:
—Who are you?
Whence do you come?
Thus, nowhere could they settle,
they were only turned away,
everywhere they were persecuted.

They stayed for a time at Coatepec,
they stayed for a time at Tollan,
they stayed for a time at Ichpuchco,
they stayed for a time at Ecatepec,
then at Chiquiuhtepetitlan.
Afterwards at Chapultepec
where many people finally settled.

And there was already an empire in Azcapotzalco,
in Coatlinchan,
in Culhuacan,
but Mexico did not yet exist.
There were still beds of rushes and reeds,
where Mexico now stands[1]

A beautiful and marvelous passage. It seems to be a guide to the interpretation of the *Boturini Codex*. The historical information, although tremendously telescoped since the events it refers to took many years, are exact. For example, the last lines. It is absolutely true that there

[1] *From the Spanish of Miguel León-Portilla.*

Coyolxauhqui, "Godess of the Moon".
Mexica Culture.

was an empire of Azcapotzalco at the time when then Aztecs arrived. Here lived the *Tecpanecas,* a group originally from the Valley of Toluca who had preserved Toltec civilization to quite a high degree. They lived in a place that had been the last stronghold of Teotihuacan culture. For a time, around 1 230, they were to rule over the Aztecs. There was also, as we saw in a preceding chapter, another old settlement (that still exists), the first Toltec capital, Culhuacan. These were two of the groups that the Aztecs encountered on arriving in the Valley of Mexico.

After the fall of Tula a great wave of nomadic tribes arrived in the south sweeping away everything in their path. Among them there was one that at the time was very unimportant, but that in time became the most powerful: the Aztecs. This tribe is sure to have taken part in the destruction of the last Toltec remains, and settled for a time in Tula, proved by the pottery found there. It was perhaps then that they made their leader into god of the Sun.

When they left Tula they were despised and exploited by everyone as they continued on their hazardous migration until, we do not know exactly how, they reached Chapultepec. They realized the strategic value of the spot and settled there for a long time, until 1299 or 1323. By then they were no longer such "savages". They had been intelligent enough to absorb progressively the culture of the peoples they had known, and also that of their neighbors since at Chapultepec they lived alongside the Culhuacanos and Tecpanecas. They had probably already learned advanced agricultural techniques like "chinampas" (floating gardens) and we know that they already had codices or painted books, a calendar, cyclical festivals and even stone buildings, however rudimentary.

But Huitzilopochtli made it his business to make them hated by their neighbors, who formed a coalition to subdue them. The Aztecs were tricked into leaving their fortified places, and taken prisoner. Their leader, Huitzilihuitl, was sacrificed at Culhuacan where the Aztecs remained captives of the Culhua. Shortly afterwards Achitometl, governor of Culhuacan gave them lands in Tizapán, south of present-day Mexico City. This was not a gracious concession but was made in the hope that the plentiful snakes there would kill off all the Aztecs. When some time afterwards Achitometl sent emissaries to see if this had in fact happened, they found the Aztecs roasting and eating the snakes. The native text says:

> *The Aztecs were overjoyed*
> *when they saw the serpents,*
> *they roasted them all*
> *they roasted them to eat them,*
> *the Aztecs ate them up*[2]

While they were at Tizapán, The Aztecs received another order from Huitzilopochtli: "Hear ye, we shall not stay here, but further on yet there are those we shall seize and dominate; yea, we shall not go fruitlessly to deal with the Culhuacanos in a friendly way, but we shall start a war; thus I command it. Therefore, go to Achitometl and ask for his offspring, his maiden daughter, his own beloved daughter; I know and I shall give her to you".

And so the Aztecs asked Achitometl for a daughter, giving him to understand that she would be made into a goddess. They said to him: "we all beg you to grant us, to give us your necklace, your quetzal feather, your maiden daughter, the noble princess our granddaughter for us to protect there in Tizapán". To which Achitometl replied: "It is well, O Mexicas, then take her". But when they returned to Tizapán, Huitzilopochtli spoke again and ordered: "Kill, flay, I order you, the daughter of Achitometl, and when she is flayed, dress one of the priests in her skin. Then go and bid Achitometl hither".

[2]*From the Spanish of Miguel León-Portilla*

The unsuspecting Achitometl accepted the invitation
and went happily to Tizapán, thinking he would find his
deified daughter. However, when the smoke of the copal
incense filling the temple cleared, he saw what the Aztecs
had done with his daughter, and according to the indigenous text:

> The lord of Culhuacan was most horrified,
> he cried out in terror,
> he called to the lords,
> to his vassals of Culhuacan,
> and said to them:
> —Who are you, O Culhuacanos?
> Do you not see they have flayed my daughter?
> Let us put them to death,
> let us kill them,
> may the evildoers die here.
>
> The battle then began,
> but then Huitzilopochtli was heard to say:
> —"I know what has happened,
> go with care,
> with caution escape from here".
>
> Those of Culhuacan pursued the Aztecs,
> threw them into the water,
> the Aztecs fled to Acatzintitlan.
> Yet still the Culhuacanos pursued them.
> But the Aztecs crossed hither,
> they came with arrow and shield,
> and for those who could not wade,
> a bridge was made
> by a woman dressed in the old-fashioned way;
> no one knew where she came from.
> When the Aztecs fled,
> when they went out to fight,

> *their children were sleeping in their cradles.*
> *a few others were crawling...*[3]

And so the Aztecs returned to wandering around the lake, in inhospitable and dangerous regions as far as a vaguely defined zone bounded by the Tecpaneca empire of Azcapotzalco and the Culhua empire of Culhuacan-Coatlinchan.

At last they settled in a miserable swamp, despised by everyone for being a place where it was practically impossible to survive except by making tremendous efforts in food-gathering and hunting. There was here however a spring that later, with the rise of Tenochtitlan, would occupy a priviledged position as the Tozpalatl, or place of magic waters.

To be able to settle in the middle of the lake, on that swampy island, another prophesy of Huitzilopochtli had to be fulfilled. They had to find an eagle perched on rocks and a cactus, eating (it is said) a snake, although the text speaks of birds. And so it was, that there among the reeds:

> *They then arrived*
> *where the cactus springs.*
> *Close by the rocks they were happy to see*
> *how an eagle stood on that cactus.*
> *There it was eating something,*
> *that it tore apart as it ate.*
> *When the eagle saw the Aztecs,*
> *it bowed its head.*
> *From afar they beheld the eagle,*
> *its nest of gorgeous many-colored feathers.*
> *Feathers of the blue bird,*
> *feathers of the red bird,*
> *all precious feathers.*
> *Also scattered there were*

[3]
From the Spanish of Miguel León-Portilla.

> *heads of divers birds,*
> *claws and bones of birds*[4]

So they decided to found the first temple to their tutelary god there. The chronicle says "...and cutting the thickest possible turves from those reed beds, they made a square base next to the very cactus to found the sanctuary, where they built a house, small and poor, in the fashion of a shrine, covered with straw from the same lake because they could not go farther afield as they were living and building in a place belonging to others, since the place they were in lay on the limits of Azcapotzalco and Texcoco, as there the lands separated from each other". The building of this temple also marks the foundation of México-Tenochtitlan, in 1325, a native year 2 House.

The Aztecs then started out on the road that was to lead them to their extraordinary power. First, subjects of the Tecpanecas of Azcapotzalco, they became their mercenaries and in 1367 helped them to destroy Culhuacan, the last place where real Toltec tribes lived. In 1371 they subjugated the other Mexica branch, which had separated from the others and lived in a place north of the Aztecs, the Tlatelolcas. They took Tenayuca, the capital of the ancient Chichimec empire of Xolotl, which had been founded in the 12th century, and five years later decided to have their own governor. They did not choose anyone from powerful Azcapotzalco, but cleverly decided to elect a descendant of the former King of Culhuacan. This first lord of the Mexica was called Acamapichtli, and through his Toltec origins the Mexica or Aztecs could claim to be heirs of the great Toltec culture and afterwards claim its heritage, which led them to the conquest of all Mesoamerica. But this still lay in the future; for the moment Acamapichtli, on orders from Azcapotzalco, declared war on the Valley of Morelos.

[4] *From the Spanish of Miguel León-Portilla.*

Tenayuca Pyramid.
Chichimeca Culture.

Also on behalf of the inhabitants of Azcapotzalco they later conquered Texcoco, the last stronghold of the Chichimec governors. Xaltocan fell first in 1400, and then it only remained for the Tecpanecas, masters of Culhuacan and Tenayuca, and governed by Tezozómoc, an extraordinary individual whose reign was to last 63 years, to conquer Texcoco. This was carried out in the reign of Ixtlilxóchitl who, to save the situation decided to abdicate in 1414 in favor of his son, one of the most extraordinary personages of Ancient Mexico, Nezahualcóyotl. He was governor, poet, mystic, notable builder, heir to Toltec and Chichimec traditions that in him fused with marvelous results.

Ixtlilxóchitl was assassinated at the very ceremony of handing over of power, and Nezahualcóyotl went into hiding until he could return to occupy his throne with the help of the Aztecs to whose governors he was related, being the nephew of Chimalpopoca, the third Aztec *Tlatoani*.

In this way the Aztecs became extraordinary warriors as mercenaries of the Tepanecas, and, as Jiménez Moreno says: "learnt at the school of Tezozomoc of Azcapotzalco".

On the death of Acamapichtli, his son Huitzilihuitl ascended the throne and continued the struggle against the people of Morelos. When he died in 1417 he was succeeded by Chimalpopoca, who through his mother was grandson of Tezozómoc of Azcapotzalco.

When Chimalpopoca died the Aztecs elected a son of Acamapichtli, Itzcóatl, and the final step was made towards the absolute freedom of the Aztecs and the initial impulse given to their empire. One, certainly historical person seems to have been responsible for all this, who was to be a sort of power behind the throne for a long period. His name was Tlacaélel, of whom the texts say:

(The Aztecs) defeated the Tecpanecas of Azcapotzalco,
those of Coyoacán and of Xochimilco
and the Cuitláhuac people.

It was Tlacaélel who rose
and fought first, and made conquest.
And only thus did he show himself
because he never wished to be supreme governor
in the city of México-Tenochtitlan,
but in fact he came to control it.
He lived happily in great plenty.

There was none so valiant
as the first, the greatest
the honored man of the realm,
the great war leader,
the most valiant Tlacaélel,
as is seen in the Annals.
It was he who managed to make
Huitzilopochtli the god of the Aztecs,
convincing them of this.[5]

Then what we have described happened. In order to put
an end to the tradition of Quetzalcóatl and finally give the
Aztecs the basis for their mystico-bellicose vision of
conquest.

His history was put away
But afterwards it was burnt:
when Itzcóatl reigned in Mexico
a decision was taken,
the Mexica lords said:
"It is not fitting that everyone
should know the paintings.

5
From the Spanish of Miguel León-Portilla.

> *Those that are our subjects (the people)*
> *will be led astray*
> *and the land will become corrupt*
> *because there many lies are preserved*[6]

This is why it is said that Izcoatl "did only what Tlacaélel advised him". Tlacaélel was half brother to the *Tlatoani* Moctezuma I, and also his advisor, and he is also said to have been counselor to Axayácatl and Tizoc. During his period of power he initiated the flower war in which the only object was to take prisoners to be sacrificed to Huitzilopochtli in the great temple of Mexico. He also granted titles of nobility to outstanding warriors, distributed lands to the king, to the lords of the recently formed nobility, and also allocated lands to each of the districts or *calpullis* in Mexico-Tenochtitlan. In other words he took the first steps towards transforming the capital into the extraordinary city that Cortés and his army were to find.

Azcapotzalco, then governed by Maxtla, fell in 1428 but Maxtla fled and took refuge in Coyoacán, which also fell, and was finally defeated in 1433. Nezahualcóyotl then returned to the throne of Texcoco where he died in 1472 after a long reign.

In 1434 the cities of Mexico, Texcoco and Tlacopan (today Tacuba) united their strength permanently to form the triple alliance, and decided to share out the booty from the conquests they would make in the future in appropriate percentages.

When Itzcoatl died in 1440 his nephew, Moctezuma I or Ilhuicamina, another great leader, ascended the throne. Under him the position of Tenochtitlan was strengthened and the so called Aztec Empire really began to take shape. He embarked on the conquest of Oaxaca and the Gulf Coast where he subjugated the Totonacs, whose rich lands became the future granary of Tenochtitlan. In fact, the conquest of this area was also prompted by an unusually

[6]*From the Spanish of Miguel León-Portilla.*

long drought, from 1450 to 1454, in Mexico, which caused a terrible famine.

Towards 1469 Axayácatl, also a descendent of Acamapichtli, ascended the throne and started conquering. A very important conquest was that of neighboring Tlatelolco, which had kept a certain measure of autonomy. Axayácatl made conquests in the Valley of Toluca and on the border of Guerrero so as to have a route for his invasion of the Tarascans, but his troops were never able to cross the River Balsas.

Tizoc, successor of Axayácatl, reigned only from 1481 to 1486, when he appears to have been poisoned. Even in this short time he managed to make numerous conquests which are shown on a magnificent monolith, the "Stone of Tizoc" now in the National Museum of Mexico. He was followed by Ahuizotl, who after reigning for one year decided to dedicate with great ceremony the Great Temple of Tenochtitlan which was now finished. He is said to have sacrificed 80,000 people on this occasion, an incredible number, certainly exaggerated, but which left and indelible memory. In addition he completed the conquest of Oaxaca and reached as far as the present border of Guatemala.

In 1502 he died in a most unbecoming way for a great conqueror. In that year a dike burst and caused a great flood in Mexico. As he was trying to escape, Ahuizotl struck his head on a lintel and died from the blow.

He was succeeded on the throne by Moctezuma II, but the long line of great Mexican conquerors and military leaders came to an end with him. This *Tlatoani,* who formerly had been famous as a great captain, became a mystic despot and dedicated himself rather to court ceremonial.

However, the 17 years of his reign were spent in continual warfare and in the quashing of the rebellions of some tribes who, driven to desperation by the Aztec oppression, rose in arms. Meanwhile, in the capital Moctezuma dedicated himself to pleasure and religious duties.

Finally, in 1519, he received the terrible news: Quetzal-cóatl had returned to take possession of the throne the emperor had been keeping for him. This marks the beginning of the Conquest, that does not fall within the scope of this book.

By this time, Tecnochtitlan, was a city of extraordinary beauty. Bernal Díaz del Castillo describes it when he tells how Moctezuma II escorted Cortés up the Great Temple of Tlatelolco so that the Conquistador could appreciate the city from the top. In his *"Historia Verdadera de la Conquista de la Nueva España"* he says:

"And then he took his hand and told him to look at his great city and all the other cities on the water and many other towns on land around the lake, and that if he had not seen the great square very well he could see it from there to great advantage. And thus we were looking at it because that great accursed temple was so high that it dominated everything; and from there we could see the three causeways leading into Mexico, which are that of Iztapalapa, by which we had entered four days previously; that of Tacuba along which we fled from the city on the night of our great defeat, when Cuedlavaca, (Cuitlahuac) drove out of the city, as we shall tell later; and that of Tepeaquilla. And we could see the fresh water that came from Chapultepec, from which the city took its supply; and on those three causeways, the bridges that were placed at intervals under which the water flowed from one part of the lake to another; and we could see in that lake a great multitude of canoes, some arriving with supplies of food and others returning with cargoes of merchandise; and we saw that every house in that great city and of all the other cities that were established on the water, from house to house the only way was by drawbridges made of wood, or in canoes; and we saw in those cities temples and shrines built in the manner of towers and fortresses, and all whitened, which was wonderful to behold, and the houses with flat roofs, and on the causeways other small towers

Xochipilli, "The Flower Prince".
Mexica Culture.

and shrines that were like fortresses. And after having looked, and considered all the things we had seen, we turned to see the great square and the multitude of people in it, some buying and others selling, so that the noise and buzz of voices and words there carried more than a league. And among us there were soldiers who had been in many parts of the world, in Constantinople, in all Italy and Rome, and they said that they had never seen a square so well proportioned and of such harmony and size and full of so many people''.

A short time afterwards, all that they admired so much was razed to its foundations by the very same Conquistadors. Even immediately after the Conquest an anonymous native poet, whose memories of this beautiful city were still fresh, wrote one of what have been called the sad chants of the Conquest:

And all this happened to us.
We saw it,
we looked upon it in wonder.
With this pitiful and sad fate
We were afflicted.

On the roads lie broken spears,
the horses are scattered.
Roofless are the houses,
Stained red their walls.

Worms swarm in the streets and squares,
and brains bespatter the walls.
Red are the waters, as if dyed,
and when we drink of them
it were as if we drank brine.

Meanwhile we struck the adobe walls,
and our reward was a net of holes.

Its safety lay in shields,
but its solitude could not be borne even with shields.

We ate colorín wood,
we chewed salty grass,
adobe bricks, lizards,
rats, powdered stone, maggots...

We ate meat
that had hardly felt the fire
When the meat was cooked,
they snatched it out,
in the very fire they ate it.
A price was put on us.
A price for the boychild, a price for the maiden.

Enough! the price for a poor man
was only two handfuls of corn,
only ten cakes of fly;
our price was only
twenty cakes of salty grass.

And all this happened to us.
We saw it,
we beheld it with wonder.
With this pitiful and sad fate,
we were afflicted[7]

So ended the glory and fame of Mexico-Tenochtitlan, and with it, that of marvelous Mesoamerica.

---

[7] *From the Spanish of Miguel León-Portilla. To make the text more dramatic we have repeated the first five lines at the end, which is not in the original text.*

Printed in:
Programas Educativos, S.A. de C.V.
Calz. Chabacano No. 65 Local A
Col. Ampliación Asturias
06850 México, D.F.
1000 ejemplares
Mexico, City. April, 1993